SPOTLIGHT

CW01046092

# TIERRA DEL FUEGO & CHILEAN PATAGONIA

WAYNE BERNHARDSON

# Contents

# TIERRA DEL FUEGO & CHILEAN PATAGONIA

# TIERRA DEL FUEGO AND CHILEAN PATAGONIA

If Patagonia is exciting, Tierra del Fuego—the "uttermost part of the earth"—is electrifying. In the days of sail, the reputation of its sub-Antarctic weather and ferocious westerlies obsessed seamen whether or not they had ever experienced the thrill—or terror—of "rounding the Horn." After Richard Henry Dana survived the southern seas en route to California in November 1834, he vividly recounted conditions that could change from calm to chaos in an instant:

> "Here comes Cape Horn!" said the chief mate; and we had hardly time to haul down and clew up, before it was upon us. In a few moments, a heavier sea was raised than I had ever seen before, and...the little brig... plunged into it, and all the forward part of her was under water; the sea pouring in through the bow ports and hawse-hole, and over the knight-heads, threatening to wash everything overboard.... At the same time sleet and hail were driving with all fury against us.

In Dana's time, that was the price of admission to one of the earth's most spectacular combinations of sea, sky, land, and ice. In a landscape whose granite pinnacles jut nearly 2,000 meters out of the ocean, only a handful of hunter-gatherers foraging in the fjords and forests could know the area with any intimacy. Today, fortunately, there are ways to reach the archipelago of Tierra del Fuego that involve less hardship—not to mention motion sickness—than Dana and his shipmates suffered.

© WAYNE BERNHARDSON

# HIGHLIGHTS

**◖ Museo Marítimo de Ushuaia:** Much more than its name suggests, Ushuaia's best museum needs more than one visit to absorb its maritime heritage and appreciate the way one of the world's most remote prisons affected the city's development (page 15).

**◖ Estancia Harberton:** East of Ushuaia, this historic *estancia* is, arguably, the nucleus of the "uttermost part of the earth" (page 25).

**◖ Glaciar Martial:** Whether entirely by foot or partly by chairlift, the climb to Ushuaia's nearby glacier, part of Parque Nacional Tierra del Fuego, rewards visitors with panoramic views of the city and the storied Beagle Channel (page 27).

**◖ Puerto Williams:** On Isla Navarino, across the Beagle Channel from Ushuaia in Chile, tiny Williams retains much of the "uttermost part of the earth" ambience that the Argentine city once offered. It also provides access to the rugged hiking trails of the Dientes de Navarino, a series of summits that rise like inverted vampire's fangs (page 33).

**◖ Casa Braun-Menéndez (Museo Regional de Magallanes):** In Punta Arenas, Chile, Magallanes's regional museum occupies what was the mansion of Patagonia's wool aristocracy (page 41).

**◖ Monumento Natural Los Pingüinos:** In the summer season, penguins occupy every square centimeter of Isla Magdalena, also home to a historic lighthouse (page 52).

**◖ Parque Nacional Pali Aike:** Hugging the Argentine border, the caves of the northern Magallanes's volcanic steppe feature some of the continent's prime early-man sites (page 55).

**◖ The Fjords of Fuegia:** It may be expensive to cruise the ice-clogged inlets of the archipelago of Tierra del Fuego, from Punta Arenas to Ushuaia, Cape Horn, and back, but it's still cheaper than chartering your own yacht. Even backpackers sometimes splurge for a leg of this unforgettable itinerary (page 57).

**◖ Torres del Paine:** The granite needles that rise above the Patagonian steppe are a beacon drawing travelers from around the world to Chile's premier national park, Parque Nacional Torres del Paine (page 74).

**◖ Cuernos del Paine:** This jagged interface between igneous and metamorphic rock, also in Parque Nacional Torres del Paine, comprises some of the world's most breathtaking alpine scenery (page 74).

LOOK FOR ◖ TO FIND RECOMMENDED SIGHTS, ACTIVITIES, DINING, AND LODGING.

In his memoirs, pioneer settler Lucas Bridges labeled Tierra del Fuego the "Uttermost Part of the Earth" for its splendid isolation at the continent's southern tip. It's still a place where fur seals, sea lions, and penguins cavort in the choppy seas of the strait named for the celebrated navigator Ferdinand Magellan, where Darwin sailed on the *Beagle* and the first 49ers found their route to California. From the seashore, behind its capital of Ushuaia, glacial horns rise like sacred steeples. The beaches and southern beech forests of Parque Nacional Tierra del Fuego, west of the city, are the terminus of the world's southernmost highway.

Tierra del Fuego is not just one island, but an archipelago, though the Isla Grande de Tierra del Fuego is South America's largest island. Chile shares the territory with Argentina; while parts of the Argentine side are urbanized, the Chilean side has just a few small towns and isolated *estancias*. Roads are few but improving, and some are now paved, especially on the Argentine side; the unpaved roads, though, can be hell on windshields, which are most cheaply replaced in the Chilean mainland city of Punta Arenas.

Two ferry routes connect the Chilean mainland to Tierra del Fuego: a shuttle from Punta Delgada, only 45 kilometers south of Argentina's Santa Cruz province, across the Primera Angostura narrows to Puerto Espora, and a daily service from Punta Arenas to Porvenir, one of the widest parts of the strait.

Chilean Patagonia's exact boundaries are imprecise because, in a sense, the region exists only in the imagination. In Chile, Patagonia has no juridical reality, though nearly everybody would agree that both Region XI (Aisén) and Region XII (Magallanes) are at least part of it. Other more northerly areas would like to be included, if only to partake of the Patagonian mystique; this chapter, though, covers only Magallanes, a popular destination in an area where travelers cross borders frequently.

Chile's most southerly region has acquired international fame thanks to the Torres del Paine, the magnificent granite needles that loom above the Patagonian plains. Pacific storms drench the nearly uninhabited western cordillera, feeding alpine and continental glaciers and rushing rivers, but rolling grasslands and seemingly unstoppable winds typify the eastern areas in the Andean rain shadow. Along the Strait of Magellan, the city of Punta Arenas is the center for excursions to a variety of attractions, including easily accessible penguin colonies and Tierra del Fuego's remote fjords. The region has no direct road connections to the rest of Chile—travelers must arrive by air, sea, or through Argentine Patagonia.

Administratively, Region XII (Magallanes) includes all Chilean territory beyond 49°S—theoretically to the South Pole, as Chile claims a slice of Antarctica between 53° and 90°W longitude. It also takes in the Chilean half of the Isla Grande de Tierra del Fuego, west of about 68°35', and most of archipelagic Tierra del Fuego.

Over the past decade, improved cross-border communications have meant that many visitors to the Argentine side also visit Chile to see Puerto Natales, Torres del Paine, and other Chilean attractions. While prices are higher in Chile than in Argentina, they are also stable and, after the initial surprise, most visitors adapt accordingly.

As in Argentina, January and February are the peak months. Prices drop in the off-season—though many places also close. Like El Calafate, the area enjoys a lengthening season.

## PLANNING YOUR TIME

Like the rest of southern South America, Tierra del Fuego and Chilean Patagonia deserve all the time you can give them, but most visitors have to make choices. On Tierra del Fuego, Ushuaia is the best sightseeing base, given its access for excursions to the nearby national park, the Beagle Channel, and Estancia Harberton, with a minimum of three days. Hikers may wish to spend several days more, and fly-fishing

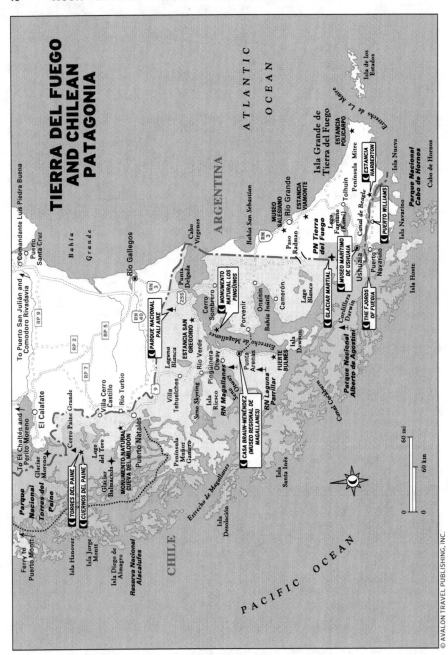

# TIERRA DEL FUEGO AND CHILEAN PATAGONIA

aficionados—who often prefer the vicinity of Río Grande—can easily stay a week or two.

Exploring Chile's thinly populated sector requires a vehicle, or even an airplane—connections to Puerto Williams, though it's not far from Ushuaia as the crow flies, are haphazard except by commercial flights from Punta Arenas. Once you're there, it takes at least a week to hike the Dientes circuit.

On the Chilean mainland, Punta Arenas can be a sightseeing base, but usually only for a day or two; for those who haven't seen Magellanic penguins elsewhere, it's worth scheduling or waiting for the boat to Isla Magdalena. Punta Arenas is also the home port for the spectacular cruise to Tierra del Fuego's remotest fjords and Cape Horn via Ushuaia, a trip that merits its full week but is worth doing even in a three- or four-day segment. Based on an island in the western Strait of Magellan, summer whale-watching is attracting a small but growing public on three-day excursions.

Puerto Natales, the urban gateway to Torres del Paine, is primarily a place to prepare for trekking, but its seaside setting, youthful exuberance, and nearby hiking excursions often extend the stay. The park deserves no less than a week, for day-hikers and overnight trekkers alike, but even a day trip—some people do it, despite the time and difficulty of getting here—is worth the trouble.

Another attraction is the *Skorpios III* cruise through the fjords on the west side of the Campos de Hielo Sur, across the ice from Torres del Paine. In the summer season, this pioneering five-day, four-night excursion could become a regional highlight.

## HISTORY

European familiarity with southernmost South America dates from 1520, when the Portuguese navigator Fernando Magalhaes, under the Spanish flag, sailed through the strait that now bears his name (Magallanes in Spanish, Magellan in English). Ranging from three to 25 kilometers in width, the strait became a maritime thoroughfare en route to the Pacific.

Prior to their "discovery" by Magellan,

southern South America's insular extremes were inhabited by hunter-gatherer bands such as the Selkn'am (Ona), Kawasqar (Alacaluf), and Yámana (Yahgan). They lived off maritime and terrestrial resources that they considered abundant—only in the European view was this a land of deprivation. The archipelago acquired its name from the fires set by the region's so-called "Canoe Indians," the Kawasqar and Yámana, for heating and cooking; in this soggy region, though, it might have been more accurate to call it Tierra del Humo (Land of Smoke).

Early navigators dreaded Cape Horn's wild seas, and their reports gave their countrymen little reason to settle in or even explore the area. In the early 1830s, Captain Robert Fitzroy of the *Beagle* abducted several Yámana, including the famous Jemmy Button, to England; he subjected them to missionary indoctrination before returning them to their home on a later voyage. On that voyage, a perplexed Charles Darwin commented on the simplicity of their society: "The perfect equality among the individuals composing the Fuegian tribes, must for a long time retard their civilization."

The first to try to bring civilization to the Yámana, rather than the opposite, were Anglican missionaries from the Falkland Islands, some of whose descendents still live here. After abortive attempts that included both Fuegian assaults and the starvation death of evangelist Allen Gardiner, the Anglican Thomas Bridges settled at present-day Ushuaia, on the Argentine side of the Isla Grande, where he compiled an English-Yámana dictionary. His son Lucas, who grew up with Yámana playmates, wrote the extraordinary memoir *The Uttermost Part of the Earth,* published a few years before his death in 1950.

In the meantime, both the Chilean and Argentine governments established their presence, and gigantic sheep *estancias* occupied the sprawling grasslands where native peoples once hunted guanaco and other game. As the guanaco slowly disappeared and the desperate Fuegians began to hunt domestic sheep, they often found themselves facing the wrong end of a rifle—though introduced European diseases such as typhoid and measles killed more native people than did bullets.

The archipelago's borders were never clearly defined, and the two countries nearly went to war over three small Beagle Channel islands in 1979. Positions were uncompromising—one Argentine poster adamantly proclaimed "We will never surrender what is ours!"—but papal mediation averted open warfare and brought a settlement within a few years. There are lingering issues, though, such as transportation across the Channel from Ushuaia to Puerto Williams.

Since then, travel to the uttermost part of the earth has boomed, especially on the Argentine side in the summer months. Other important economic sectors are sheep farming and petroleum, on both the Chilean and Argentine sides.

## Chilean Patagonia

Some of the oldest archaeological evidence for human habitation on the entire continent comes from Magallanes, from volcanic rock shelters in and near Parque Nacional Pali Aike along the Argentine border. Pleistocene hunter-gatherers once stalked now-extinct species such as giant ground sloths and native American horses, but later adopted more broad-spectrum forms of subsistence that included marine and coastal resources. These peoples were the predecessors of today's few surviving Tehuelche and Kawasqar (Alacaluf) peoples, and the nearly extinct Selkn'am (Ona) and Yámana (Yahgan) who gathered shellfish on the coast and hunted guanaco and rhea with bows and arrows and *boleadoras*.

Spain's 16th-century colonization attempts failed miserably, as did the initial Chilean and Argentine efforts, but the city of Punta Arenas finally took hold after 1848—thanks largely to the fortuitous discovery of gold in California just a year later. Gold fever soon subsided, but the introduction of sheep brought a wool and mutton boom that benefited from the Franco-Prussian War of the 1870s, and helped create sprawling *estancias* that dominated the region's political, social, and economic life for nearly a century.

While the livestock industry hangs on, commercial fisheries, the state-run oil industry, and the tourist trade have superseded it in the regional economy. Even these industries, though, have proved vulnerable to fluctuations, declining reserves, and international developments beyond their control, but Magallanes is presently one of Chile's most prosperous areas. The Zona Franca free-trade zone that once fueled the regional economy, even drawing immigrants from central Chile, has stagnated but is still significant.

# Ushuaia

Beneath the Martial range's serrated spires, on the Beagle Channel's north shore, the city of Ushuaia is both an end (virtually the terminus of the world's southernmost highway) and a beginning (the gateway to Antarctica). The surrounding countryside is increasingly popular with activities-oriented visitors who enjoy hiking, mountain biking, fishing, and skiing.

After more than two decades of economic growth and physical sprawl, the provincial capital is both declining and improving. On the one hand, the duty-free manufacturing, fishing, and tourist boom that transformed a onetime penal colony and naval base into a bustling city has weakened. On the other, it's begun to spruce up the waterfront and restore historic buildings that gave the town its personality, some of them becoming hotels or bed-and-breakfasts. The streets are cleaner (though the main Avenida San Martín is tourist-trap ugly) and there are more parks, plazas, and green spaces. Still, Ushuaia has serious particulate pollution problems because high winds kick up dust in the unpaved streets of its newer neighborhoods.

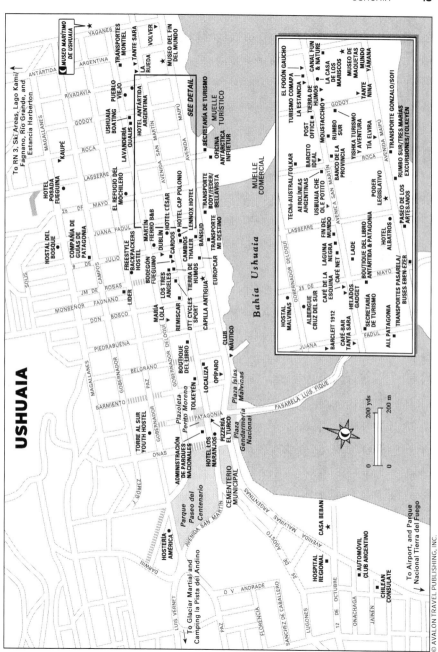

USHUAIA

© AVALON TRAVEL PUBLISHING, INC.

## HISTORY

Ushuaia dates from 1870, when the Anglican South American Missionary Society decided to place the archipelago's first permanent European settlement here. Pioneer missionary Thomas Bridges and his descendants have left an enduring legacy in Bridges' Yámana (Yahgan) dictionary, his son Lucas's memoir, and the family *estancia* at nearby Harberton (sadly, the Yahgans whom Thomas Bridges hoped to save succumbed to introduced diseases and conflict with other settlers).

Not long after Ushuaia's settlement, Argentina, alarmed by the British presence, moved to establish its own authority at Ushuaia and did so with a penal settlement for its most

## BOUND FOR THE ICE

Since the Soviet Union's demise, Ushuaia has become the main jumping-off point for Antarctic excursions on Russian icebreakers that, despite being chartered under U.S. officers, sometimes still show the hammer and sickle on their bows. For travelers with flexible schedules, it's sometimes possible to make last-minute arrangements at huge discounts – no ship wants to sail with empty berths – for as little as US$1,500. Normal rates, though, are around US$3,000 or more for 9-14 days, including several days' transit across the stormy Drake Passage – medication is advisable.

If your timing is bad and budget cruises are not available, many Ushuaia travel agencies can make alternative arrangements. The season runs mid-November-mid-March.

On the waterfront Muelle Comercial, Ushuaia's **Oficina Antártida Infuetur** (tel. 02901/424431, antartida@tierradelfuego. org.ar) has the latest information on Antarctic cruises. Guidebooks to the white continent include Jeff Rubin's *Antarctica* (Lonely Planet, 2005), Ron Naveen's *Oceanites Site Guide to the Antarctic Peninsula* (Chevy Chase, MD: Oceanites, 1997), and the third edition of Tony Soper and Dafila Scott's *Antarctica: A Guide to the Wildlife* (Bradt Publications, 2000).

© WAYNE BERNHARDSON

former Soviet research icebreaker, now an Antarctic cruise ship, in Ushuaia

infamous criminals and political undesirables. It remained a penal settlement until almost 1950, when Juan Domingo Perón's government created a major naval base to support Argentina's claim to a share of Antarctica. Only since the end of the 1976–1983 military dictatorship has it become a tourist destination, visited by countless cruise ships as well as overland travelers and air passengers who come to see the world's southernmost city.

Stretching east–west along the Beagle Channel's north shore, Ushuaia (pop. 64,107, an almost 40 percent increase over the 2001 census) is 3,220 kilometers south of Buenos Aires and 190 kilometers southwest of Río Grande, the island's only other city.

## SIGHTS

Even if it's leveled off, Ushuaia's economic boom provided the wherewithal to preserve and even restore some of the city's historic buildings. Two of them are now museums: Dating from 1903, the waterfront **Casa Fernández Valdés** (Avenida Maipú 175) houses the historical Museo del Fin del Mundo, while the 1896 **Presidio de Ushuaia** (Yaganes and Gobernador Paz) is now the misleadingly named Museo Marítimo (while not insignificant, its maritime exhibits are less interesting than those on the city's genesis as a penal colony).

Three blocks west of the Casa Fernández Valdés, dating from 1894, the classically Magellanic **Poder Legislativo** (Maipú 465) once housed the provincial legislature; it's now open to the public 10 A.M.–8 P.M. weekdays, 3–8 P.M. weekends. Five blocks farther west, prisoners built the restored **Capilla Antigua** (Avenida Maipú and Rosas), a chapel dating from 1898. The municipal tourist office occupies the **Biblioteca Sarmiento** (1926), the city's first public library, at San Martín 674. At the west end of downtown, the waterfront **Casa Beban** (Avenida Malvinas Argentinas and 12 de Octubre) is a reassembled pioneer residence dating from 1913; it now houses the municipal Casa de la Cultura, a cultural center.

## Museo del Fin del Mundo

Benefiting greatly from exterior restoration of its block-style construction, Ushuaia's evolving historical museum contains improved exhibits on the Yámana, Selkn'am, and other Fuegian Indians, and on early European voyages. There remain permanent exhibits on the presidio, the Fique family's El Primer Argentino general store, the original branch of the state-run Banco de la Nación (which occupied the building for more than 60 years), and natural history, including run-of-the-mill taxidermy. Its celebrity artifact is one of few existing copies of Thomas Bridges' Yámana-English dictionary.

An open-air sector includes representations of a Yámana encampment and dwellings, plus machinery used in early agriculture and forestry projects. The Museo del Fin del Mundo (Avenida Maipú 175, tel. 02901/421863, www.tierradelfuego.org.ar/museo) also contains a bookstore/souvenir shop and a specialized library on southernmost Argentina, the surrounding oceans, and Antarctica. The exceptional website places much of this material online.

November–April, hours are 9 A.M.–8 P.M. daily, with guided tours at 10 A.M., noon, and 2 and 5 P.M.; the rest of the year, hours are noon–7 P.M. daily except Sunday, with guided tours at 2 and 5 P.M. daily. Admission costs US$3.50 for adults, US$2 for students and retired people, and is free for children 14 and under. There is no additional charge for tours.

## ◀ Museo Marítimo de Ushuaia

Misleadingly named, Ushuaia's maritime museum (Yaganes and Gobernador Paz, tel. 02901/437481, museomar@satlink.com) most effectively tells the story of Ushuaia's inauspicious origins as a penal settlement for both civilian and military prisoners. Alarmed over the South American Missionary Society's incursions among the indigenous peoples of the Beagle Channel, Argentina reinforced its claims to the territory by building, in 1884, a military prison on Isla de los Estados (Staten Island), across the Strait of Lemaire at the southeastern tip of the Isla Grande.

Barely a decade later, in 1896, it established Ushuaia's civilian Cárcel de Reincidentes for repeat offenders; after finally deciding, in 1902, that Isla de los Estados was a hardship station even for prisoners, the military moved their own facility to Ushuaia. Then, in 1911, the two institutions fused in this building that, over the first half of the 20th century, held some of the country's most famous political prisoners, celebrated rogues, and notorious psychopaths.

Divided into five two-story pavilions, with 380 cells intended for one prisoner each, the prison held as many as 600 prisoners at a time before closing in 1947. Its most famous inmates were political detainees such as immigrant Russian anarchist Simón Radowitzsky, who killed Buenos Aires police chief Ramón Falcón with a bomb in 1909; Radical politicians Ricardo Rojas, Honorio Pueyrredón, and Mario Guido (the deceptively named Radicals are in fact an insipid and ineffectual middle-class party); and Peronist politician Héctor Cámpora, who was briefly president in the 1970s.

Many if not most prisoners, though, were long-termers or lifers such as the diminutive strangler Cayetano Santos Godino, a serial killer dubbed "El Orejudo" for his oversized ears (interestingly enough, the nickname also describes a large-eared bat that is native to the archipelago). Julio Ordano has written a play, performed in Buenos Aires, about Santos Godino, *El Petiso Orejudo.*

Life-size figures of the most infamous inmates, modified department store dummies clad in prison stripes, occupy many cells. One particularly interesting exhibit is a wide-ranging comparison with other prisons that have become museums, such as San Francisco's Alcatraz and South Africa's Robben Island.

The museum does justify its name with an exceptional exhibit of scale models of ships that have played a role in local history, such as Magellan's galleon *Trinidad,* the legendary *Beagle,* the South American Missionary Society's three successive sailboats known as the *Allen Gardiner,* and Antarctic explorer and conqueror Roald Amundsen's *Fram.* In addition, there are materials on Argentina's Antarctic presence since the early 20th century, when the corvette

*Uruguay* rescued Otto Nordenskjöld's Norwegian expedition, whose crew included the Argentine José María Sobral. On the grounds is a full-size replica of the Faro San Juan de Salvamento, the Isla de los Estados (Staten Island) lighthouse that figures in Jules Verne's story "The Lighthouse at the End of the World."

In addition, this exceptional museum contains a philatelic room, natural history exhibits, and admirable accounts of the region's aboriginal peoples. In fact, it has only two drawbacks: There's too much to see in a single day, and the English translations could use some polishing—to say the least.

The Museo Marítimo is open 9 A.M.–8 P.M. daily from mid-October to the end of April; the rest of the year, it opens an hour later. Guided tours are at 11:30 A.M. and 6:15 P.M. daily, but schedules can change.

Admission costs US$7 per person but, on request, the staff will validate your ticket for another day; since there's so much here, splitting up sightseeing sessions is a good idea. There are discounts for children under age six (US$1.50), students and senior citizens (both US$2), and families (US$12 including up to four children). It has an excellent book and souvenir shop, and a fine *confitería* for snacks and coffee.

## Museo de Maquetas Mundo Yámana

While both the Museo del Fin del Mundo and Museo Marítimo do a creditable job on Tierra del Fuego's indigenous heritage, this small private museum (Rivadavia 56, tel. 02901/422874, mundoyamana@infovia.com.ar) consists of skillfully assembled dioramas of life along the Beagle Channel prior to the European presence, at a scale of 1:15. It also includes cartographic representations of the Yámana and their neighbors, interpretations of the European impact, and panels of historical photographs.

Open 10 A.M.–8 P.M. daily, the Museo de Maquetas Mundo Yámana charges US$2.50 per person for adults, US$1.25 for students and retired people, and is free for children under 13. The staff speak fluent English.

# ENTERTAINMENT

Ushuaia has sprouted a plethora of pubs, some but not all with Irish aspirations or pretensions, such as **Dublin** (9 de Julio 168), with a standard menu of *minutas* (short orders). More strictly Argentine is **Ushuaia Che Que Potito** (San Martín 471), with eclectic decor, a menu that's a step above pub grub (the lightly fried *rabas*, or squid rings, are excellent), and live music on weekends (starting around 1:30 A.M.).

# SHOPPING

The **Boutique del Libro Antártida & Patagonia** (25 de Mayo 62, tel. 2901/432117, www.antartidaypatagonia.com.ar) carries a wide choice of Argentine and imported books, in Spanish, English, and other languages, on the "uttermost part of the earth" and its surroundings, including current Moon Handbooks at reasonable prices; there are also novels for that long voyage across the Drake Passage to Antarctica. Its other **Boutique del Libro** (San Martín 1129, tel. 02901/424750) offers an excellent selection of Spanish-language books and a smaller choice of English-language titles.

Along with many similar venues along Ushuaia's main shopping street, **Fin del Mundo** (San Martín 505, tel. 02901/422971) has many kitschy souvenirs but also maps and books. Nearby **Laguna Negra** (San Martín 513, tel. 02901/431144) specializes in locally produced chocolates.

**Tierra de Humos** (San Martín 246 and San Martín 861) stocks locally produced leather, fleeces, handicrafts, and silverwork. For purchases directly from the artisans, there's the open-air **Paseo de los Artesanos** (Maipú and Lasserre), at the entrance to the Muelle Comercial (port).

# ACCOMMODATIONS

Ushuaia has abundant accommodations, but it's long been one of the most expensive destinations in what was, until recently, an expensive country. Demand is also high, though, in the summer months of January and February, when prices rise and reservations are advisable. One heartening development is the proliferation of good but moderately priced backpacker hostels and the arrival of several bed-and-breakfasts—known by the semi-English acronym ByB—some of them excellent alternatives.

## Under US$10

Eight kilometers west of Ushuaia on the Lapataia road, the **Camping Municipal** has free but limited facilities (fire pits and pit toilets only). A stiff climb to the northwest of downtown, **La Pista del Andino** (Alem 2873, tel. 02901/435890 or 02901/15-568626, www.lapistadelandino.com.ar, US$3 pp) has slightly sloping sites at its ski area; the first transfer from downtown or the airport is free. Guests with sleeping bags can crash in the *refugio* above its bar/restaurant, but shouldn't expect to get to sleep early.

## US$10-25

Perched at downtown's western edge, with spectacular Beagle Channel views, HI affiliate **Torre al Sur Youth Hostel** (Gobernador Paz 1437, tel. 02901/430745, www.torrealsur.com.ar, US$7–8 pp) has been one of Argentina's finest backpacker facilities, but overcrowding and noise have gotten it mixed recent reviews. Rooms have two or four beds, with lockers; there's hot water, Internet access, and free luggage storage.

The HI affiliate **Albergue Los Cormoranes** (Kamshen 788, tel. 02902/423459, www.loscormoranes.com, US$7–8 pp with breakfast) has attractive common areas, including a wind-sheltered garden, and arguably better sleeping facilities than Torre al Sur. Most easily reached by climbing Don Bosco to its end and then taking a left, it's about eight steep blocks north of the waterfront (arrival transfers are free).

The more central **Albergue Cruz del Sur** (Deloqui 636, tel. 02901/434099, www.xdelsur.com.ar, US$8 pp) is an independent hostel with four-, six-, or eight-bed rooms; there is also cable TV, Internet access, two kitchens, and a free initial pickup. Guests also get a series of discounts and specials at various services around town.

Nearby **El Refugio del Mochilero** (25 de Mayo 241, tel. 02901/436129, www.refugio delmochilero.netfirms.com, US$8 pp) has almost equally good facilities but a little less ambience than it once had.

Half a block from the Lider bus terminal, **Freestyle Backpackers Hostel** (Gobernador Paz 866, tel. 02901/432874, www.ushuaiafree style.com, US$10 pp, US$47 d with breakfast) is a gleaming new purpose-built hostel with a youthful ambience, a spacious lounge and kitchen facilities, and secondary amenities including laundry service and parking. The more expensive rooms are doubles with private bath.

## US$25-50

**Pueblo Viejo** (Deloqui 242, tel. 02901/432098, www.puebloviejo.info, US$33/45 s/d with shared bath) is a new bed-and-breakfast on the foundations of an early Ushuaia house; replicating the traditional Magellanic style, it's added innovative contemporary touches. The street-level rooms are more luminous than their semi-basement counterparts.

On the hillside, the more contemporary **◖ Martín Fierro B&B** (9 de Julio 175, tel. 02901/430525, javiersplace@hotmail.com, US$35/50 s/d) has two bunks in each of several small but well-designed rooms with shared baths. Host Javier Jury has created tasteful common areas that are simultaneously spacious and cozy, and the breakfast is varied and filling; the tiny shower stalls, though, make bathing with a friend impossible without being *really* intimate. Two downstairs "aparthotel" rooms (US$80) sleep up to four people each.

## US$50-100

Rehabbed **Hotel César** (San Martín 753, tel. 02901/421460, www.hotelcesarhostal.com.ar, US$40/60 s/d) has become one of the central area's better values.

**Hostal Malvinas** (Gobernador Deloqui 615, tel./fax 02901/422626, www.hostalmalvinas .net, US$50/60 s/d) provides simple but quiet and immaculate rooms with large baths and no frills—not even TV—but croissants and coffee are free all day.

In addition to moderately priced rooms, **Hotel Antártida Argentina** (Rivadavia 172, tel. 02901/435761, www.antartidahotel.com .ar, US$63 s or d) has a promising upscale restaurant.

Responsive **Hostería América** (Gobernador Paz 1665, tel. 02901/423358, www .hosteriaamerica@arnet.com.ar, US$60/73 s/d) is a decent choice in a fine location above the Parque Paseo del Centenario.

## US$100-200

Hillside **Hotel Ushuaia** (Lasserre 933, tel. 02901/430671, www.ushuaiahotel.com.ar, US$80/110 s/d with breakfast) is a good value in its price range.

Only its busy location detracts from the bright and cheerful **Hotel Cap Polonio** (San Martín 746, tel. 02901/422140 or 02901/422131, www.hotelcappolonio.com.ar, US$110 s or d). All rooms are carpeted, with cable TV; the private baths have tubs as well as showers, and there's a good restaurant/*confitería* with breakfast included.

At the west end, one of Ushuaia's tallest buildings, the brand-new **Hotel Los Naranjos** (San Martín 1446, tel. 02901/435862, www .losnaranjosushuaia.com, US$119 s or d) offers comfortable midsize rooms with either channel or glacier views, at least from the uppermost floors. The restaurant menu is worth a look.

**Hostal del Bosque** (Magallanes 709, tel./ fax 02901/430777 or 02901/421723, www .hostaldelbosque.com.ar, US$120 s or d) is an "aparthotel" whose two-room suites, with kitchenette, can sleep up to four people. There are large baths, with shower and tub, and cable TV; it also has its own restaurant.

The spacious **Hotel Albatros** (Avenida Maipú 505, tel. 02901/433446, www.albatros hotel.com.ar, US$160 s or d) is the pick of the waterfront accommodations.

From its cul-de-sac perch, **◖ Hotel Posada Fueguina** (Lasserre 438, tel. 02901/423467, www.posadafueguina.com.ar, US$97/130–123/163 s/d) offers awesome views plus cable TV, and similar amenities, and has added *cabañas* to handle any overflow.

Downtown's new **Lennox Hotel** (San Martín 776, tel./fax 02901/436430, www .lennoxhotel.com.ar, US$170 s or d) has mid-size rooms with either channel or mountain views, but even with amenities such as whirlpool tubs and WiFi it's hard to think it's nearly triple the price of, say, Hotel César.

In dense woods about 1.5 kilometers northeast of downtown, **Patagonia Villa Lodge** (Bahía Buen Suceso 563, tel. 02901/435937, www.patagoniavilla.com, US$190 s or d) has just four rooms in luminous semi-detached cabins with a magnificently rustic architecture and comforts such as whirlpool tubs (in some, at least) and WiFi. There is one darker double (US$95) that suffers only by comparison with the others; elsewhere, it would count among the best in town. Owner Luciana Lupotti, a former Florida exchange student, speaks fluent English. Rates include airport pickup/drop-off.

The interior is more impressive than the surprisingly plain exterior at the luxury **Hotel del Glaciar** (Luis Martial 2355, tel. 02901/430640, www.hoteldelglaciar.com, US$189–199 s or d). At Km 3.5 on the road to the Martial glacier, each room has either a mountain or ocean view, but it's questionable whether staffing is sufficient for a hotel of its category—and price.

## Over US$200

At Km 3 on the glacier road, the **[ Hotel y Resort Las Hayas** (Luis Martial 1650, tel. 02901/430710, www.lashayas.com.ar, US$262 s or d) enjoys nearly all conceivable luxuries, including an elaborate buffet breakfast, gym, sauna, whirlpool tub, and a heated indoor pool; it picks up guests at the airport, and offers a regular shuttle to and from downtown. Behind its surprisingly utilitarian exterior, some of its 93 rooms and suites suffer from hideous decor—the wallpaper is to cringe at—but all are comfortable and its staff are highly professional.

## FOOD

Ushuaia has always been an expensive place to eat, but the 2002 peso collapse reined in prices.

That said, there are still some truly expensive choices; the financially challenged should look for *tenedor libre* specials, or be cautious with extras like dessert and coffee.

Hotel Cap Polonio's **Marcopolo** (San Martín 730, tel. 02901/430001) is a café-restaurant that serves excellent coffee, chocolate, and croissants for breakfast—try the *submarino* for a cold morning's pickup. **Café de la Esquina** (San Martín 602, tel. 02901/423676) is a popular meeting place with similar offerings, as well as sandwiches for late-afternoon tea.

Open for lunch only weekdays, but with Saturday evening hours, **Pizzería El Turco** (San Martín 1440, tel. 02901/424711) is good and moderately priced, but it lacks the variety found at the slightly more expensive **Opíparo** (Avenida Maipú 1255, tel. 02901/434022), which also serves pasta dishes. Well-established **Barcleit 1912** (Fadul 148, tel. 02901/433105) seems to have fallen a step behind some of the other pizzerias, but also has a variety of moderately priced short orders.

One of Ushuaia's finest, **[ Tante Sara** (San Martín 137, tel./fax 02901/435005) serves outstanding pasta with a broad selection of imaginative sauces, as well as pizza, but the kitchen and service can both be slow and it's become noisier. Most entrées, such as ravioli with king crab, fall into the US$5–7 range, with sauces extra. For breakfast, coffee, sandwiches, and desserts, try their **Café-Bar Tanta Sara** (San Martín 701, tel. 02901/423912).

In an artfully restored historic house, **Bodegón Fueguino** (San Martín 859, tel. 02901/431972) specializes in Fuegian lamb, prepared in a variety of styles for around US$8, but it also has seafood dishes, tangy beef empanadas, and good desserts.

**Barcito Ideal** (San Martín 393, tel. 02901/437860) seems always to draw crowds to its US$8 *tenedor libre* buffet. **La Rueda** (San Martín 193, tel. 02901/436540) charges only slightly more for its own buffet *parrillada*. Nearby **La Estancia** (San Martín 253, tel. 02901/436540) and **El Fogón Gaucho** (San Martín 237, tel. 02901/430100) have similar fare. The well-established **Moustacchio** (San

Martín 298, tel. 02901/423308) stresses seafood but also serves beef and other meats.

Ushuaia has a wider choice of seafood restaurants than almost any other Argentine provincial city. **La Casa de los Mariscos** (San Martín 232, tel. 02901/421928) specializes in *centolla* (king crab), but also has many other fish and shellfish options in the US$5–10 range. Looking like a *porteño* antiques shop housed in a classic Magellanic residence, tango-themed **Volver** (Avenida Maipú 37, tel. 02901/423977) doesn't quite live up to its potential—the fish and seafood dishes, such as *abadejo al ajillo* (US$7) and king crab soup (US$4), are disappointingly bland. With a 30-year history, **Tante Nina** (Gobernador Godoy 15, tel. 02901/432444) focuses on Fuegian fish and seafood, but also serves Patagonian lamb and "homely pasta."

Other possibilities include the **El Náutico** (Avenida Maipú and Belgrano, tel. 02901/430415), where entrées start around US$6; **Tía Elvira** (Avenida Maipú 349, tel. 02901/424725), where four-course dinners cost around US$12–14; and **◖ Kaupé** (Roca 470, tel. 02901/422704), which serves an exclusively (and exclusive) à la carte menu. The latter has specialties such as king crab (US$13), exquisite lemon ice cream, carpaccio, and wine by the glass. Even post-devaluation, a full meal here costs upwards of US$25, but it's worth the splurge.

Equally top-of-the-line—both literally and geographically—is the dining-with-a-panoramic-view at **◖ Chez Manu** (Luis Martial 2135, tel. 02901/423253), immediately below the Hotel del Glaciar. Using local ingredients such as king crab and lamb, the French-run restaurant is *the* place for a truly elaborate meal at equally elaborate prices: US$25 and up. Along with Kaupé, this is one Ushuaia restaurant with food to match its views.

**Amaranto Bistrot** (Rivadavia 172, tel. 02901/435761), the restaurant for Hotel Antártida, has visions of joining that elite group. While it's promising and there are many intriguingly cosmopolitan menu items, it's not there yet—but it's also cheaper than either Chez Manu or Kaupé.

On a promontory, in a recycled building that once transmitted Argentina's first ever color TV program—the 1978 World Cup—**María Lola** (Deloqui 1048, tel. 02901/421185) may be Ushuaia's best new restaurant. Items such as Fuegian trout (US$13) and a wild-boar sandwich with Gruyère and red peppers on a braided roll (US$6) suggest the menu's diversity, and the bar serves a variety of mixed drinks for US$4–5 each. Open for lunch and dinner, it's closed Monday.

**Helados Gadget** (San Martín 621) has all the conventional Argentine ice cream flavors—good enough in their own right—but also incorporates regional specialties such as *calafate* and, occasionally, rhubarb.

## INFORMATION

Ushuaia's well-organized municipal **Secretaría de Turismo** (San Martín 674, tel. 02901/424550, www.e-ushuaia.com) is open 8 A.M.–10 P.M. weekdays and 9 A.M.–8 P.M. weekends and holidays. English-speaking staff are normally present.

There's a subsidiary office at the **Muelle Turístico** (tel. 02901/437666), open 8 A.M.–6 P.M. daily, and another at the airport (tel. 02901/423970) that's open for arriving flights only.

The provincial **Instituto Fueguino de Turismo (Infuetur)** has ground-floor offices at Hotel Albatros (Avenida Maipú 505, tel. 02901/423340, info@tierradelfuego.org.ar).

Motorists can consult the **Automóvil Club Argentino** (ACA, Malvinas Argentinas and Onachaga, tel. 02901/421121).

The **Administración de Parques Nacionales** (APN, San Martín 1395, tel. 02901/421315, tierradelfuego@apn.gov.ar) is open 9 A.M.–noon weekdays.

At the waterfront Muelle Comercial, the **Oficina Antártica Infuetur** (tel. 02901/421423, antartica@tierradelfuego.org.ar) has the latest information on Antarctic sailings and tours. Hours are 8 A.M.–5 P.M. daily in summer, 9 A.M.–4 P.M. weekdays the rest of the year.

## SERVICES

Several banks have ATMs, including **BanSud** (Avenida Maipú 781) and **Banco de la Provincia** (San Martín 396); the latter accepts travelers checks at a 3 percent commission. **Cambio Thaler** (San Martín /88, tel. 02901/421911) also takes 3 percent on travelers checks but keeps longer hours: 9:30 A.M.–1:30 P.M. and 4–8 P.M. weekdays, 10 A.M.–1:30 P.M. and 5:30–8 P.M. Saturday, and 5:30–8 P.M. Sunday.

**Correo Argentino** (San Martín 309) is the post office; the postal code is 9410.

**Café Net** (San Martín 565, tel. 02901/422720) provides telephone, fax, and Internet access, including erratically available WiFi. **Contacto II** (San Martín 838) is a good alternative, though it lacks WiFi.

The **Chilean consulate** (Jainén 50, tel. 02901/430970) is open 9 A.M.–1 P.M. weekdays.

The **Dirección Nacional de Migraciones** (Beauvoir 1536, tel. 02901/422334) is open 9 A.M.–5 P.M. weekdays.

**Los Tres Angeles** (Juan Manuel de Rosas 139, tel. 02901/422687) offers quick and reliable laundry service, but can be overwhelmed in high season; try instead **Lavanderías Qualis** (Deloqui 368, tel. 02901/421996).

The **Hospital Regional** (tel. 02901/422950, 107 for emergencies) is at Maipú and 12 de Octubre.

## GETTING THERE

Ushuaia has good air connections to Buenos Aires and intermediate points, and improving overland transportation from mainland Argentina and from Chile. Maritime transportation is either tenuous or expensive.

### Air

**Aerolíneas Argentinas** (Roca 116, tel. 02901/421218) normally flies two or three times daily to Aeroparque, sometimes via Río Gallegos, El Calafate, or Trelew. Occasional Buenos Aires–bound flights land at the international airport Ezeiza instead of Aeroparque.

The Chilean carrier LAN flies several times weekly to Punta Arenas, Chile—Ushuaia's only scheduled international service—while its local affiliate LAN Argentina serves Aeroparque and other destinations. As LAN has no local office, it's necessary to purchase tickets from travel agencies or over the Internet.

In the Galería Albatros, **LADE** (San Martín 564, Local 5, tel. 02901/421123) flies irregularly to Río Gallegos, El Calafate, Comodoro Rivadavia, Bariloche, and Buenos Aires.

For Puerto Williams, across the Channel in Chile, it may be possible to arrange a private charter through the **Aeroclub Ushuaia** (tel. 02901/421717 or 02901/421892) for about US$100 per person.

### Bus

Ushuaia lacks a central bus terminal. **Lider** (Gobernador Paz 921, tel. 02901/436421) goes to Tolhuin (US$5, 1.5 hours) and Río Grande (US$10, 3.5 hours) eight times daily except Sunday and holidays, when it goes only six times. **Transportes Montiel** (Deloqui 110, tel. 02901/421366) goes to Tolhuin and Río Grande six or seven times daily except Sundays and holidays, when it goes five times only.

**Tecni-Austral** (Roca 157, tel. 02901/431408) goes daily at 5:30 A.M. to Río Grande, sometimes continuing to Río Gallegos (US$32, 12 hours) and others to Punta Arenas, Chile (US$35, 12 hours).

### Sea

The Chilean cruisers MV *Mare Australis* and *Vía Australis* offer luxury sightseeing cruises to Puerto Williams, Cape Horn, and through the fjords of Chilean Tierra del Fuego to Punta Arenas; while not intended as simple transportation, they can serve the same purpose for those who can afford them. It's possible to either disembark in Punta Arenas (four days) or return to Ushuaia (in a week). These cruises are usually booked far in advance, but on occasion—normally just before Christmas—it may be possible to make on-the-spot arrangements.

Political complications between Chile and Argentina continue to complicate regular transportation across the Beagle Channel to Puerto Williams, even though in December 2001 the two countries agreed to open Puerto Navarino, at the east end of Isla Navarino, as a port of entry to Chile. Nevertheless, **Ushuaia Boating** (Godoy 190, tel. 02901/436193, www.ushuaiaboating.com.ar) occasionally shuttles passengers across the Channel to Puerto Williams (US$100 pp, two hours).

## GETTING AROUND
### To the Airport
A causeway links the city with **Aeropuerto Internacional Malvinas Argentinas,** which has the country's highest airport taxes: US$5 for elsewhere in Argentina, and US$20 for international flights. Taxis and *remises* cost only about US$2–3 pp with **Remiscar** (San Martín 995, tel. 02901/422222, www.remiscar.com.ar).

### Bus
Several bus companies all charge around US$7–8 round-trip per person to Parque Nacional Tierra del Fuego; it's normally possible to camp in the park and return the following day. Note that the companies below, as indicated, use several different stops along the waterfront, but do not have offices there; some have telephones and others do not. The schedules below are summer hours that may change; at other seasons, schedules are reduced.

From Avenida Maipú and 25 de Mayo, **Transporte Pasarela** (tel. 02901/433712) and **Buses Eben-Ezer** (tel. 02901/431133) have 18 buses daily to the park between 8 A.M. and 7 P.M., returning between 9 A.M. and 8 P.M.

From Maipú and Fadul, **Body** and **Feder** go 17 times daily between 8:30 A.M. and 7 P.M., returning between 9:30 A.M. and 8 P.M.

From Maipú and Roca, **Gonzalo** operates six buses daily between 9:30 A.M. and 4 P.M., returning between 10:30 A.M. and 7:30 P.M.

From Maipú and 9 de Julio, **Mi Destino** has a dozen departures between 9 A.M. and 7 P.M., returning between 9:45 A.M. and 8 P.M. From Maipú and Lasserre, **Lautaro** goes to the park at 9:15 and 11:15 A.M., and at 6:15 P.M. daily except Sunday, returning at 10 A.M., noon, and 7:30 P.M.

Mi Destino, Gonzalo, and Body have several services daily to the chairlift at the Glaciar Martial (US$3 pp), normally with a minimum of two passengers.

Body and Bellavista, both at Maipú and Fadul, each have a 10 A.M. departure for Estancia Harberton (US$23 pp round-trip); Body returns at 4 P.M., Bellavista at 5 P.M. Gonzalo and Sofi, both at Maipú and Roca, go to Harberton at 9 A.M. and 2:30 P.M., respectively, returning at 4 P.M. and 5 P.M.

### Car and Bicycle Rental
Car rentals start around US$23 per day and range up to US$200 per day for four-wheel-drive vehicles. Some agencies offer unlimited mileage within Tierra del Fuego Province, but others limit this to as few as 50 kilometers per day, so verify before signing any contract.

Rental agencies include **Cardos** (San Martín 845, tel. 02901/436388, cardosr@hotmail.com), **Europcar** (Maipú 857, tel./fax 02901/430786, europcar@carletti.com.ar), **Hertz** (at the airport, tel. 02901/432429, hertzushuaia@infovia.com.ar), and **Localiza** (San Martín 1222, tel. 02901/430739, localizaushuaia@yahoo.com.ar).

**DTT Cycles Sport** (San Martín 903, tel. 02901/434939) rents mountain bikes.

# Vicinity of Ushuaia

Ushuaia has more than a dozen travel agencies offering excursions in and around Ushuaia, ranging from double-decker-bus city tours (US$7, one hour) to Parque Nacional Tierra del Fuego (US$17, 4–5 hours) and historic Estancia Harberton (US$55–120, eight hours). They also organize activities such as hiking, climbing, horseback riding, fishing, and mountain biking.

Local operators include **All Patagonia** (Juana Fadul 60, tel. 02901/433622, fax 02901/430707, www.allpatagonia.com), which is the AmEx representative; **Canal Fun & Nature** (Rivadavia 82, tel. 02901/437395, www.canalfun.com); **Rumbo Sur** (San Martín 342, tel. 02901/422441, fax 02901/430699, www.rumbosur.com.ar); **Tolkar** (Roca 157, Local 1, tel. 02901/431408, www.tolkar turismo.com.ar); **Tolkeyén** (San Martín 1267, tel. 02901/437073, www.tolkeyenpatagonia .com); and **Yishka Turismo y Aventura** (Gobernador Godoy 62, tel./fax 02901/437606, yishka@speedy.com.ar).

The **Compañía de Guías de Patagonia** (Gobernador Campos 795, tel. 02901/437753, www.companiadeguias.com.ar) specializes in trekking.

## BEAGLE CHANNEL BOAT EXCURSIONS

From the Muelle Turístico, at the foot of Lasserre, there are boat trips to Beagle Channel

## UNLEASHING THE BEAGLE

In 1978, military dictatorships in Chile and Argentina barely avoided war over three small islands in the Beagle Channel. Though successive civilian governments have resolved the territorial dispute, ease of movement across the channel is still not what it could – or should – be.

According to the Chilean viewpoint, the Argentines have failed to live up to their part of the 1978 agreement, which implied reciprocal border openings at Agua Negra (between the Argentine city of San Juan and the Chilean city of La Serena) for Argentina and Puerto Almanza (opposite Puerto Williams) for Chile. For the Chileans, it's also a matter of principle that, as they provide overland access to Argentine Tierra del Fuego through Chilean territory, the Argentines should reciprocate with access to Isla Navarino for them.

This sounds reasonable enough, but at the same time Argentina's federal government (unlike Chile, which is a unitary state) has to deal with elected provincial authorities still obsessed with territoriality, as well as Ushuaia business interests who fear a loss of commerce to flyspeck Puerto Williams. In

reality, improved communications would probably encourage more tourists to stay longer in the area, and Puerto Williams shoppers to take advantage of Ushuaia's better goods and lower prices.

In early 2001, at the invitation of the Chilean navy, President Ricardo Lagos paid a visit to Puerto Williams in the company of Sernatur head Oscar Santelices and Argentine ambassador Daniel Olmos, but there have still been no concrete transportation developments between Williams and Puerto Almanza. In December of that year, though, Chile declared Puerto Navarino a port of entry for Chilean-flagged vessels, permitting day excursions from Ushuaia to the southern Beagle Channel fjords.

Because excursionists would have to stay in Argentina, there were hopes that this step would help satisfy Ushuaia interests who, apparently, worry that Puerto Williams might undermine Ushuaia's claim to be the world's southernmost city. Reportedly, a Chilean businessman purchased a catamaran for this purpose, but no further movement has taken place. Still, the situation bears watching.

© WAYNE BERNHARDSON

view of the Beagle Channel from Glaciar Martial, Parque Nacional Tierra del Fuego

wildlife sites such as **Isla de los Lobos,** home to the southern sea lion (*Otaria flavescens*) and the rarer southern fur seal (*Arctocephalus australis*), and **Isla de Pájaros,** a nesting site for seabirds, mostly cormorants. These excursions cost around US$20–33 per person for a 2.5-hour trip on oversized catamarans such as the *Ana B, Ezequiel B,* and *Luciano Beta.* With extensions to the penguin colony at Estancia Harberton and a visit to the *estancia* itself, the cost is about US$50.

Rumbo Sur and Tolkeyén sell tickets for these excursions from offices at the foot of the Muelle Turístico, where Héctor Monsalve's **Tres Marías Excursiones** (tel./fax 02901/421897, marias3@satlink.com) operates four-hour trips (US$30–35 pp) on a smaller vessel (eight passengers maximum) that can approach Isla de Lobos more closely than the large catamarans. They also land on Isla Bridges, a small but diverse island with cormorant colonies, shell mounds, and even the odd penguin.

## FERROCARRIL AUSTRAL FUEGUINO

During Ushuaia's early days, prison labor built a short-line, narrow-gauge steam-driven railroad west into what is now Parque Nacional Tierra del Fuego to haul the timber that built the city. Only a few years ago, commercial interests rehabilitated part of the roadbed to create a gentrified, antiseptic tourist version of the earlier line that pretty much ignores the unsavory aspects of its history to focus on the admittedly appealing forest scenery of the Cañadón del Toro.

The train leaves from the **Estación del Fin del Mundo** (tel. 02901/431600, fax 02901/437696, www.trendelfindelmundo.com.ar), eight kilometers west of Ushuaia at the municipal campground. October–mid-April, there are three departures daily, while the rest of the year there are only one or perhaps two if demand is sufficient. The two-hour-plus excursion costs US$18 per person in tourist class, US$35 per person in first class, and US$75–100 per person with a buffet lunch or dinner.

## SKIING

Ushuaia gets most of its visitors in summer, but it's becoming a winter sports center as well, thanks to its proximity to the mountains. Downhill skiing, snowboarding, cross-country skiing, and even dogsledding are possibilities.

The major ski event is mid-August's **Marcha Blanca,** which symbolically repeats Argentine liberator José de San Martín's heroic winter crossing of the Andes from Mendoza to assist his Chilean counterpart Bernardo O'Higgins against the Spaniards. Luring upwards of 400 skiers, it starts from the Las Cotorras cross-country area and climbs to Paso Garibaldi, the 430-meter pass between the Sierra Alvear and the Sierra Lucas Bridges. Ideally, it takes place August 17, the anniversary of San Martín's death (Argentine novelist Tomás Eloy Martínez has called his countrymen "cadaver cultists" for their apparent obsession with celebrating death rather than birth dates of their national icons).

There are two downhill ski areas. The aging **Centro de Deportes Invernales Luis Martial** (Luis Martial 3995, tel. 02901/15-613890 or 02901/15-568587, esquiush@tierradelfuego.org.ar), seven kilometers northwest of town at the end of the road, has a single 1,130-meter run on a 23-degree slope, with a double-seat chairlift capable of carrying 224 skiers per hour.

East of Ushuaia, **Cerro Castor** (RN 3 Km 27, www.cerrocastor.com) has up-to-the-minute facilities, including four lifts and 15 different runs. In mid-season, lift tickets cost US$23–33 per day, with discounts for multiday packages; in low and shoulder seasons, there are additional discounts.

Otherwise areas east of town, along RN 3, are for cross-country skiers. These include **Tierra Mayor** (Km 21, tel. 02901/437454, tierramayor@tierradelfuego.org.ar), **Las Cotorras** (Km 26, tel. 02901/499300), **Haruwen** (Km 35, tel./fax 02901/424058, haruwen@tierradelfuego.org.ar), and several newer options. All of them rent equipment and offer transfers from Ushuaia.

## ◀ ESTANCIA HARBERTON

Historic Harberton dates from 1886, when missionary pioneer Thomas Bridges resigned from Ushuaia's Anglican mission to settle at his new *estancia* at Downeast, later renamed for the Devonshire home town of his wife, Mary Ann Varder. Thomas Bridges, of course, was the author of the famous English-Yámana dictionary, and their son Lucas continued the family literary tradition with *The Uttermost Part of the Earth*, an extraordinary memoir of a boyhood and life among the indigenous Yámana and Ona (Selkn'am).

Harberton continues to be a family enterprise—its present manager and part-owner, Tommy Goodall, is Thomas Bridges' great-grandson. While the wool industry that spawned it has declined in recent years (though it has about 1,000 cattle), the *estancia* has opened its doors to organized English- and Spanish-language tours of its grounds and outbuildings; these include the family cemetery, flower gardens, woolshed, woodshop, boathouse, and a native botanical garden whose

© WAYNE BERNHARDSON

Estancia Harberton

Yámana-style lean-tos are far more realistic than their Disneyfied counterparts along the Ferrocarril Austral Fueguino tourist train. Photographs in the woolshed illustrate the process of cutting firewood by axes and transporting it by raft and oxcart, and the tasks of gathering and shearing sheep.

In addition, American biologist Rae Natalie Prosser (Tommy Goodall's wife) has also created the **Museo Acatushún de Aves y Mamíferos Marinos Australes** (www.acatushun .com, US$2 pp), a bone museum stressing the region's marine mammals but also seabirds and a few shorebirds; it's open 10 A.M.–7 P.M. daily mid-October–mid-April. It's also possible to visit Magellanic penguin rookeries at Isla Martillo (Yecapasela) with Pira Tour for US$18 per person; a small colony of gentoo penguins has recently established itself on the island, making this a more intriguing trip for those who've seen Magellanic penguins elsewhere.

Estancia Harberton (tel. 02901/422742, fax 029091/422743 in Ushuaia, ngoodall@ tierradelfuego.org.ar) is 85 kilometers east of Ushuaia via paved RN 3 and gravel RC-j, but work has stopped on a new coastal road from Ushuaia that would shorten the distance.

Mid-October–mid-April, the *estancia* is open for guided tours (US$4 pp) 10 A.M.–7 P.M. daily except Christmas, New Year's, and Easter. Note that because of Harberton's isolation there is no telephone and email communications can be slow, as they require a trip to Ushuaia.

With written permission, **camping** is permitted at unimproved sites; the *estancia* has also remodeled the former cookhouse (two rooms with 4–5 beds each and shared bath) and shepherds' house (two rooms of three beds with private bath), which are available for US$60–80 d, depending on the room.

Harberton's **Casa de Té Mánacatush** provides full board for US$30 pp, and also serves a tasty afternoon tea (US$4.50 pp) for nonguests.

In summer, several companies provide round-trip transportation from Ushuaia (US$20–30 pp), but services change frequently. From Ushuaia's Muelle Turístico, Piratur (tel. 02901/15-604646) offers a US$50 package with overland transportation and a visit to the penguin colony.

Catamaran tours from Ushuaia are more expensive and spend less time at Harberton, but do include the farm-tour fee.

# Parque Nacional Tierra del Fuego

For pilgrims to the uttermost part of the earth, mecca is Parque Nacional Tierra del Fuego's Bahía Lapataia, where RN 3 ends on the Beagle Channel's north shore. It's a worthy goal but, sadly, most visitors see only the area in and around the highway because most of the park's mountainous interior, with its alpine lakes, limpid rivers, blue-tinged glaciers, and jagged summits, is closed to public access.

## GEOGRAPHY AND CLIMATE

About 18 kilometers west of Ushuaia, Parque Nacional Tierra del Fuego hugs the Chilean border as its 63,000 hectares stretch from the Beagle Channel north across Lago Fagnano

(Kami). Elevations range from sea level on the channel to 1,450 meters on the summit of Monte Vinciguerra.

Most of the park has a maritime climate, with frequent high winds. Rainfall is moderate at about 750 millimeters per annum, but humidity is fairly high, as relatively low temperatures inhibit evapotranspiration—the summer average is only about 10°C. The record maximum temperature is 31°C, while the record minimum is a fairly mild -12°C. At sea level, snow rarely sticks for long, but at higher elevations there are permanent snowfields and glaciers.

## FLORA AND FAUNA

As in southernmost Chile, thick southern beech forests cover the Argentine sector of Tierra del Fuego. Along the coast, the deciduous *lenga* (*Nothofagus pumilio*) and the Magellanic evergreen *coigüe* (*Nothofagus betuloides*) are the main tree species; at higher elevations, the stunted, deciduous *ñirre* (*Nothofagus antarctica*) forms nearly pure stands. In some low-lying areas, where cool annual temperatures inhibit complete decomposition, dead plant material compresses into *sphagnum* peat bogs with a cover of ferns and other moisture-loving plants; the insectivorous *Drosera uniflora* swallows unsuspecting bugs.

Until recently Argentina's only coastal national park, Parque Nacional Tierra del Fuego has a seashore protected by thick kelp beds that serve as incubators for fish fry. Especially around Bahía Ensenada and Bahía Lapataia, the shoreline and inshore waters swarm with cormorants, grebes, gulls, kelp geese, oystercatchers, flightless and flying steamer ducks, snowy sheathbills, and terns. The maritime black-browed albatross skims the Beagle's waters, while the Andean condor sometimes soars overhead. Marine mammals, mostly sea lions but also fur seals and elephant seals, cavort in the ocean. The rare southern sea otter (*Lutra felina*) may exist here.

Inland areas are fauna-poor, though foxes and guanacos are present in small numbers. The most conspicuous mammals are the European rabbit (*Oryctolagus cunniculus*) and the Canadian beaver (*Castor canadiensis*), both of which were introduced for their pelts but have proved to be pests.

## HIKING

Where freshwater Lago Roca drains into the sea at Bahía Lapataia, the park's main sector has several short nature trails and a handful of longer ones; most of the backcountry is off-limits to casual hikers. Slightly less than one kilometer long, the **Senda Laguna Negra** uses a boardwalk to negotiate boggy terrain studded with ferns, wildflowers, and other water-tolerant species. The 400-meter **Senda de los Castores** (Beaver Trail) winds among southern beeches gnawed to death to form dams and

ponds where the beavers themselves occasionally peek out of their dens.

The five-kilometer **Senda Hito XXIV** follows Lago Roca's northeastern shore to a small obelisk that marks the Chilean border. If, someday, Argentine and Chilean authorities can get it together, this would be an ideal entry point to the wild backcountry of Estancia Yendegaia, but at present it's illegal to continue beyond the marker. From a junction about one kilometer up the Hito XXIV trail, **Senda Cerro Guanaco** climbs four kilometers northeast up the Arroyo Guanaco to the 970-meter summit of its namesake peak.

From Bahía Ensenada, near the park's southeastern edge, there are boat shuttles to **Isla Redonda** (US$15 pp) 10 A.M.–5:30 P.M.

## ◖ GLACIAR MARTIAL

Technically within park boundaries, but also within walking distance of Ushuaia, the Glaciar Martial is the area's best single hike, offering expansive views of the Beagle Channel and across to the jagged peaks of Chile's Isla Navarino. Reached not by RN 3 but rather by the zigzag Camino al Glaciar (also known as Luis Martial) that climbs northwest out of town, the trailhead begins at the Aerosilla del Glaciar, the ski area's chairlift, which operates 9 A.M.–7 P.M. daily. The 1.2-kilometer chairlift (US$5 pp) reduces the two-hour climb to the foot of the glacier by half. In summer there are frequent buses to the lift (US$2.50–3 round-trip) with Pasarela, Eben Ezer, and Bellavista from the corner of Avenida Maipú and 25 de Mayo, 9 A.M.–9 P.M. Though easy to follow, the trail—especially the middle segment—is steep, and the descent requires particular caution because of loose rocks and soil. There is no admission charge to this sector of the park.

## ACCOMMODATIONS AND FOOD

Camping is the only option in the park itself, where there are free sites with little or no infrastructure at **Camping Ensenada, Camping Río Pipo, Camping Las Bandurrias, Camping Laguna Verde,** and **Camping Los Cauquenes.** While these are improving, they're less tidy than the commercial **Camping Lago Roca** (tel. 02901/433313, lagoroca@speedy.com.ar, US$2–3 pp), whose more expensive "A" sector has hot showers, a grocery, and the restaurant/ *confitería* **La Cabaña del Bosque.**

## INFORMATION

At the park entrance on RN 3, the APN has a Centro de Información where it collects a US$6.50 pp entry fee. Argentine residents pay half.

Several books have useful information on Parque Nacional Tierra del Fuego, including William Leitch's *South America's National Parks* (Seattle: The Mountaineers, 1990), which is now out of print; the fifth edition of Tim Burford's *Backpacking in Chile & Argentina* (Bradt Publications, 2001); and the third edition of Clem Lindenmayer and Nick Tapp's *Trekking in the Patagonian Andes* (Lonely Planet, 2003). The latter two are hiking guides, but locals criticize the Lonely Planet guide vociferously for inaccuracy.

Bird-watchers may want to acquire Claudio Venegas Canelo's *Aves de Patagonia y Tierra del Fuego Chileno-Argentina* (Punta Arenas: Ediciones de la Universidad de Magallanes, 1986), Ricardo Clark's *Aves de Tierra del Fuego y Cabo de Hornos* (Buenos Aires: Literature of Latin America, 1986), or Enrique Couve and Claudio Vidal Ojeda's bilingual *Birds of the Beagle Channel* (Punta Arenas: Fantástico Sur Birding & Nature, 2000).

# Río Grande and Vicinity

Most visitors who stay in and around Río Grande, on the Isla Grande's blustery Atlantic shoreline, do so for the fishing. For the rest, this once desolate city is more a transit point than a destination in itself, but thanks to smoothly paved streets, the huge dust clouds that once blew through the wool and oil town have subsided. There are limits to beautification, though, as all the trees planted in Plaza Almirante Brown are stiffly wind-flagged.

Bus schedules used to dictate that travelers pass the night here, but recent improvements mean quicker connections to Ushuaia for overland travelers. Still, services have improved, and there's enough to do that an afternoon spent here need not be a wasted one.

On the north bank of its namesake river, Río Grande (pop. 52,786) is 79 kilometers southeast of the Chilean border post at San Sebastián and 190 kilometers northeast of Ushuaia via RN 3, which is now completely paved (though some deteriorating segments south toward Tolhuin will soon need repaving).

## SIGHTS

Río Grande's **Museo de La Ciudad Virginia Choquintel** (Alberdi 553, tel. 02962/430647, free admission) does a lot with a little, with good materials on natural history, surprisingly sophisticated exhibits on ethnology and aboriginal subsistence, and historic displays on maps and mapmaking, the evolution of island communications, and astronomy. Now occupying the former storehouses of the Asociación Rural de Tierra del Fuego, the Museo de la Ciudad is open 9 A.M.–8 P.M. weekdays and 3–7 P.M. Saturday.

Río Grande has few architectural landmarks—or few buildings of any antiquity for that matter—but the **Obras Sanitarias** waterworks tower (Lasserre 386), at the Plaza's northeast corner, dates from the Juan Perón era (circa 1954).

## ENTERTAINMENT

**El Cine 1 & 2** (Perito Moreno 211, tel. 02962/ 433260) shows current films in modern facilities, but sometimes turns up the volume to excruciating levels—bring or improvise ear plugs, just in case.

## ACCOMMODATIONS

Accommodations are few, particularly at the budget end, but improving. Nearly every mid- to upscale place offers a 10 percent discount for cash payment.

Río Grande's first backpackers' hostel, at the south end of town, **Hotel Argentino** (San Martín 64, tel. 02964/422546, hotelargentino@hotmail.com, US$10 pp) gets high marks for hospitality, good beds, and good common areas including kitchen access, but a couple rooms are rundown and it sometimes suffers water shortages. They'll fetch guests from the bus terminals for free.

The simple but spotless, family-run **Hospedaje Noal** (Obligado 557, tel. 02964/427516, US$8 pp, US$20d) has spacious rooms with shared bath but plenty of closet space and good beds, and some rooms with private bath. **Hotel Rawson** (Estrada 750, tel. 02964/430352, US$12 pp, US$20 d) has slipped a notch, but next-door **Hostería Río Grande** (Estrada 756, tel. 02964/425906, US$22/28 s/d) is a worthy alternative with private bath and breakfast. Possibly Río Grande's best value for money, rehabbed **Hotel Villa** (San Martín and Espora, tel. 02964/424998, US$30/34 s/d with cash discount) has cheerful contemporary rooms and assiduous service.

Around the corner from the former bus terminal, the seaside **Hotel Isla del Mar** (Güemes 936, tel. 02964/422883, fax 02964/427283, isladelmar@arnet.com.ar, US$32/38 s/d) is frayed, rather than just worn around the edges, with loose doorknobs, scuffed walls, and slowly eroding wooden built-ins. Still, it exudes a certain funky charm, even if "seaview" is a relative term here—with Río Grande's enormous tidal range, the Atlantic tides sometimes seem to be on the distant horizon. Rates include breakfast, and there's a cash discount.

Beds are softer than some might prefer in the aging but tidy rooms at **Hotel Federico Ibarra** (Rosales 357, tel. 02964/430071, hotelibarra@netcomb bs.com.ar, US$36/44 s/d), but it's worth consideration with breakfast and a 10 percent cash discount. A glass palace that looks out of place here, **Hotel Atlántida** (Avenida Belgrano 582, tel./fax 02964/431914, atlantida@netcombbs.com.ar, US$39/44 s/d) has decent rooms, but it's also well worn.

Río Grande's most professional operation, **⟨ Posada de los Sauces** (Elcano 839, tel. 02964/432895, info@posadadelossauces.com, US$42/52–54/67 s/d) is easily the top of the line. One of the suite bathrooms is large enough for a hot-tub party, and the restaurant is far away the city's most elegant.

## FOOD

**La Nueva Piamontesa** (Belgrano and Mackinlay, tel. 02964/424366) is a longstanding favorite for varied and delicate baked empanadas and the pizzas in its deli. An inexpensive sit-down restaurant as well, it's open 24/7.

Two other places specialize in pizza and pasta: **Café Sonora** (Perito Moreno 705, tel. 02964/423102) and **La Nueva Colonial** (Fagnano 669, tel. 02964/425353).

**Leymi** (25 de Mayo 1335, tel. 02964/421683) serves fixed-price lunches for about US$3.50, and has a broad menu of *parrillada*, pasta, and other short orders. **El Rincón de Julio** (Elcano 805, tel. 02964/15-604261) is a hole-in-the-wall *parrilla,* highly regarded by locals, with lunch counter–style service.

By Río Grande standards, **Araucas** (Rosales 566, tel. 02964/425919) has a sophisticated menu—a wide variety of seafood, for instance, and the Patagonian lamb (US$6) can come with variations such as a mint sauce. The desserts are excellent.

**Mamá Flora** (Avenida Belgrano 1101, tel. 02964/424087) is a good breakfast choice that also has coffee and exquisite chocolates. At the plaza's northwest corner, **Limoncello** (Rosal and Fagnano, tel. 02964/420134) is an exceptional ice creamery.

Several upscale hotels have their own restaurants, most notably the **⟨ Posada de los Sauces** (Elcano 839, tel. 02964/430868), which deserves special mention for superb service, the cooked-to-order *lomo a la pimienta* (pepper steak, US$8), and their complimentary glass of wine. There's also a 10 percent cash discount.

## INFORMATION

Río Grande's municipal **Oficina de Información Turística** (Rosales 350, tel.

02964/431324, rg-turismo@netcombbs.com. ar) is a kiosk on Plaza Almirante Brown; open 9 A.M.–9 P.M. daily in summer, 9 A.M.–8 P.M. weekdays and 10 A.M.–5 P.M. Saturday the rest of the year, it's exceptionally helpful.

The provincial **Instituto Fueguino de Turismo** (Infuetur, Espora 533, tel. 02962/422887) is open 9 A.M.–6 P.M. weekdays.

## SERVICES

**Cambio Thaler** (Rosales 259, tel. 02964/421154) is the only exchange house. Banks with ATMs include **Banco de Tierra del Fuego** (San Martín 193) and **Banca Nazionale del Lavoro** (San Martín 194).

**Correo Argentino** (Rivadavia 968) is two blocks west of San Martín; the postal code is 9420. **Locutorios del Sur** (San Martín 170) has long-distance services and Internet access.

**El Lavadero** (Perito Moreno 221) handles the washing.

For medical services, contact the **Hospital Regional** (Ameghino s/n, tel. 02964/422088).

## GETTING THERE

**Aerolíneas Argentinas** (San Martín 607, tel. 02964/422748) flies daily to Río Gallegos and Buenos Aires. **LADE** (Lasserre 425, tel. 02964/422968) flies with some frequency to Río Gallegos, less frequently to Comodoro Rivadavia.

Since the old terminal recently closed, bus companies now have their own offices, some of them shared. **Lider** (Perito Moreno 635, tel. 02964/420003) and **Transportes Montiel** (25 de Mayo 712, tel. 02964/420997) have multiple departures to Tolhuin (US$5, 1.5 hours) and Ushuaia (US$10, four hours). **Bus Sur** (Perito Moreno 635, tel. 02964/425644) goes to Punta Arenas, Chile (US$18, eight hours), Wednesday, Friday, and Sunday at 10 A.M.

**Tecni-Austral** (Moyano 516, tel. 02964/430610) goes to Punta Arenas Monday, Wednesday, and Friday at 9:30 A.M., to Río Gallegos (US$20, eight hours) via Chile daily except Sunday at 9 A.M., and to Ushuaia (US$9, four hours) daily at 4 P.M.

## GETTING AROUND

City bus Línea C goes directly to **Aeropuerto Internacional Río Grande** (tel. 02964/420600), a short distance west of downtown on RN 3, for US$0.50. It's also a reasonable cab ride.

**Europcar** (Avenida Belgrano 423, tel. 02964/432022) rents cars and pickup trucks.

## VICINITY OF RÍO GRANDE

As the area surrounding Río Grande does not have a well-developed transport infrastructure, hiring a vehicle is worth consideration.

### Reserva Provincial Costa Atlántica de Tierra del Fuego

From Cabo Nombre, at the north end of Bahía San Sebastián, to the mouth of the Río Ewan southeast of Río Grande, the Isla Grande's entire shoreline is a bird sanctuary because of the abundant plovers and sandpipers, some of which migrate yearly between the Arctic and South America. Near the San Sebastián border post is the privately owned **Refugio de Vida Silvestre Dicky,** a prime wetland habitat of 1,900 hectares.

### Misión Salesiana

One exception to Río Grande's lack of historic sites is the Salesian mission (RN 3 Km 2980, tel. 02964/421642, www.misionrg .com.ar), founded by the order to catechize the Selkn'am; after the aboriginals died out from unintentionally introduced diseases and intentional slaughter, the fathers turned their attention to educating rural youth in their boarding school. The well-preserved **Capilla** (chapel), a national historical monument, and similar Magellanic buildings comprise part of the mission's **Museo de Historia, Antropología y de Ciencias Naturales,** whose facilities display their natural history and ethnography exhibits far better than in the not-too-distant past.

From Río Grande, Línea B goes hourly to the Misión Salesiana, about 11 kilometers

Fishing for Atlantic salmon, brown trout, and rainbow trout is a popular pastime throughout Argentine Tierra del Fuego, but rules are a little intricate. There are separate licenses for Parque Nacional Tierra del Fuego and for the rest of the island, and fees differ for provincial residents, other Argentines, and foreigners.

For the park, licenses are available only from the Administración de Parques Nacionales (APN) in Ushuaia; rates are US$5 per day or US$20 per season (Nov.–mid-Apr.) for residents. For Argentines who do not live in Tierra del Fuego or foreigners, rates are US$11 per day, US$53 per week, or US$71 per season. Children under age 18 pay US$3.50 and retired Argentine citizens pay nothing.

For fishing beyond park boundaries, daily rates vary depending on the river, but range US$17-34 for foreigners; there's a 15-day license for US$34-67, and seasonal rates are US$67-133. Fuegian and Argentine residents pay a fraction of these rates.

In Ushuaia, licenses are available at the **Asociación Caza y Pesca** (Maipú 822, tel. 02901/423168, cazpescush@infoviar.com.ar) or **Óptica Eduardo's** (San Martín 830, tel. 02901/433252). In Río Grande, contact the **Club de Pesca John Goodall** (Ricardo Rojas 606, tel. 02964/424324).

RC-c, is the site of the world's largest shearing shed.

Also Sociedad Explotadora property, **Estancia José Menéndez,** 25 kilometers southwest of town via RN 3 and RC-b, is one of the island's most historic ranches. RC-b continues west to an obscure summer border crossing at **Radman,** where few visitors of any kind cross the line to Lago Blanco on the Chilean side.

For potential overnighters, though, the Sea View Guest House at the Simon and Carolina Goodall family's **Estancia Viamonte** (tel. 02964/430861, www.estanciaviamonte.com, US$100/165 s/d for bed and breakfast, US$150 pp with full board and activities) is the only place on the island that can offer the opportunity to sleep in Lucas Bridges's bedroom. Directly on RN 3, about 42 kilometers southeast of Río Grande, it fronts on a bird-rich beach; the house itself can sleep up to six people with two shared baths, plus living and dining rooms. There are extensive gardens, and chances for fishing, riding, and farm activities.

directional signs in Puerto Williams, Isla Navarino, Chilean Tierra del Fuego

north of Río Grande, from 7:30 A.M.–8:30 P.M. The museum is open 10 A.M.–12:30 P.M. and 3–7 P.M. daily except Sunday, when it keeps afternoon hours only; admission costs US$1 for adults, US$0.50 for children.

### Historic *Estancias*

Several of the region's largest and most important *estancias* are in the vicinity of Río Grande. Founded by the Menéndez dynasty's Sociedad Explotadora de Tierra del Fuego, **Estancia María Behety,** 17 kilometers west via gravel

## Lago Fagnano (Kami)

Named for the priest who spearheaded the Salesian evangelical effort among the Selkn'am, this elongated body of water fills a structural depression that stretches across the Chilean border to the west. Also known by its Selkn'am name, Kami, its shoreline is nearly 200 kilometers long and its surface covers nearly 600 square kilometers.

The lake's most westerly part, along the Chilean border, lies within Parque Nacional Tierra del Fuego but is virtually inaccessible except by boat. As might be expected, the lake is popular with fishing enthusiasts.

At the moment, since the closure of Hostería Kaikén at the east end of the lake, the main accommodations this side of Ushuaia are at Lago Escondido's **Hostería Petrel** (RN 3 Km 3186, tel. 02901/433569, petrel@arnet.com.ar, US$47 d), which has lake-view rooms with whirlpool tubs and a restaurant that's a popular stopover for tour groups.

At the east end, about midway between Río Grande and Ushuaia, pilgrims pause at the town of **Tolhuin** to sample the goods at ◖ **Panadería la Unión** (www.panaderia launion.com), a legendary bakery whose celebrity visitors have ranged from ex-president Carlos Menem to folk-rocker León Gieco, hard-rockers Los Caballeros de la Quema, and actress China Zorrilla. It has the usual fine bread but also loads of *facturas* (pastries), *alfajores,* and sandwiches; what it lacks, astonishingly for Argentina, is any coffee other than machine-dispensed instant.

For a full meal, there's nearby **La Posada de los Ramírez** (Avenida de los Shelk'nam 411, tel. 02901/492382), which has excellent pastas at bargain prices, but also meats and, on occasion, local specialties such as trout.

---

# THE FALKLAND ISLANDS (ISLAS MALVINAS)

In 1982, Britain and Argentina fought a 10-week war over the isolated Falkland Islands (which Argentines claim as the Malvinas), ending in a decisive British victory that derailed a brutal military dictatorship. The territorial dispute has not disappeared, but in the interim the islands have become an important destination for a select group of international travelers interested primarily in sub-Antarctic wildlife.

What the Falklands can offer, 500 kilometers east of the continent in the open South Atlantic, is six species of penguins, including the uncommon king and gentoo, marine mammals including elephant seals, sea lions, and fur seals, enormous nesting colonies of black-browed albatrosses and several species of cormorants. Most of these are not easily seen on the continent, and some would normally require a trip to Antarctica.

For several years after the war, the only way to reach the islands was an expensive Royal Air Force flight from England, but for the last several years LAN has offered Saturday flights to and from Punta Arenas; one flight per month picks up and drops off passengers in the Argentine city of Río Gallegos. Cruise ships pay frequent visits in the southern summer as well.

Despite their small population, only about 2,500, the islands have good tourist infrastructure in the capital of Stanley and at wildlife sites in offshore island farms that resemble Argentine and Chilean *estancias*. The big drawback is that most, though not all, of these sites are only accessible by expensive air taxis.

Because of complicated logistics, Falklands-bound visitors should consider arranging an itinerary in advance to take maximum advantage of their time – accommodations are relatively few and internal flights have limited capacity. Contact **International Tours and Travel** (P.O. Box 408, Stanley, Falkland Islands, tel. 500/22041, www.falklandstravel.com).

For further information, consult *Moon Patagonia,* which has a detailed chapter on the Falklands, and the Falkland Islands Tourist Board's thorough, well-organized website (www.tourism.org.fk).

# Chilean Tierra del Fuego

## ◖ PUERTO WILLIAMS

On Isla Navarino's north shore, across the Beagle Channel from Argentine Tierra del Fuego, Puerto Williams is the so-called "Capital of Antarctica" and gateway to the rugged Los Dientes backcountry circuit, a difficult five-day slog through soggy mountainous terrain. Local residents look forward to establishment of a permanent ferry link to nearby Argentina, but there is much political opposition across the channel because myopic Ushuaia impresarios fear losing business to tiny Williams—however unlikely that possibility.

Founded in the 1950s, formerly known as Puerto Luisa, the town (pop. 1,952) has paved sidewalks but gravel streets. Most of its residents are Chilean naval personnel living in relatively stylish prefabs, but there are also some 60 remaining Yámana descendents, only a few of whom speak the language—now a hybrid including many Spanish and English words—among themselves.

### Sights

Overlooking the harbor is the **Proa del Escampavía Yelcho,** the prow of the cutter which, at the command of Luis Pardo Villalón, rescued British Antarctic explorer Edward Shackleton's crew from Elephant Island, on the Antarctic Peninsula, in 1916. A national monument, the bow survived collisions with icebergs to get to its destination; returning to Punta Arenas, the entire ship makes a cameo appearance in original newsreel footage in British director George Butler's *Endurance,* an extraordinary documentary of the Shackleton expedition.

Very professional for a small-town museum, Williams's **Museo Martín Gusinde** (Aragay 1) has small exhibits on geology, economic plants and taxidermy, a marker for the former post office, and a sign for the coal mine at Caleta Banner, on nearby Isla Picton, which provisioned the *Yelcho* on its mission to rescue Shackleton's crew. Admission costs US$1.75 per person; hours are 9 A.M.–1 P.M. and 2:30–7 P.M. weekdays and 2–6 P.M. weekends. Nearby is the **Parque Botánico Omora,** an organized selection of native plants.

Built in Germany for operations on the Rhine, the **MV *Micalvi*** shipped supplies between remote *estancias* and other settlements before sinking in Puerto Williams' inner harbor in 1962; the upper deck and bridge remain as the yacht club's bar/restaurant.

### Accommodations, Food, and Nightlife

At **Residencial Pusaky** (Piloto Pardo 242, tel. 061/621116, US$16–20 pp), rates vary according to shared or private bath. **Refugio Coirón** (Ricardo Maragaño 168, tel. 061/621227, fax 061/621150, coiron@simltd.com, US$33/46 s/ d) has very good accommodations with kitchen privileges and shared bath.

The top choice is the 24-room **Hotel Lakutaia** (tel. 061/621733, www.lakutaia.cl, US$200/250 s/d), which was once rundown but has been utterly transformed. As the base for excursions in and around Puerto Williams, it is more a destination than just accommodations. It also has a fine restaurant. Off-season rates (May–mid-October) are about 25 percent lower.

South America's southernmost bar/restaurant, the **Club de Yates Micalvi,** occupies the main deck and the bridge of the historic vessel that lies grounded in Puerto Williams's inner harbor.

The **Pingüino Pub** is at the Centro Comercial.

### Services

Nearly all of Puerto Williams's services are concentrated around the Centro Comercial, a cluster of storefronts just uphill from the Muelle Guardián Brito, the main passenger pier. These include the post office, several telephone offices, Banco de Chile, the Cema-Chile crafts shop, and Manualidades, which rents mountain bikes. You may not be able to find an ATM in town, but make sure you have some Chilean pesos, which are essential.

## Getting There

**DAP** (tel. 061/621051), at the Centro Comercial, flies 20-seat Twin Otters to Punta Arenas (US$64) Tuesday, Thursday, and Saturday April–October. The rest of the year, flights leave daily except Sunday. DAP flights are often heavily booked, so make reservations as far in advance as possible.

Regular connections between Puerto Williams and Ushuaia, on Argentine Tierra del Fuego, continue to be problematical, but hitching a lift across the channel with a yacht is feasible—for a price. For up-to-date information, contact the **Gobernación Marítima** (tel. 061/621090), the **Club de Yates** (tel. 061/621041, int. 4250), or **Turismo Sim** (tel. 061/621150). There are occasional charter flights as well.

In summer, the **ferry** *Patagonia* sails to Punta Arenas (38 hours) Friday at 7 P.M. Fares are US$150 in a bunk, US$120 for a reclining seat.

## VICINITY OF PUERTO WILLIAMS

The Williams-based, German-Venezuelan **Sea & Ice & Mountains Adventures Unlimited** (Austral 74, tel. 061/621227, tel./fax 061/621150, www.simtld.com) organizes trekking, climbing, and riding expeditions on Isla Navarino and the Cordillera Darwin, week-long yacht excursions around the Beagle Channel and to Cape Horn, and even Antarctica. Advance booking is essential.

## The Coastal Road

From Puerto Williams, a coastal road runs 54 kilometers west to the village of Puerto Navarino, now a legal port of entry, and 28 kilometers east to Caleta Eugenia; only two kilometers east of Williams, **Villa Ukika** is the last refuge of the Yámana. From Caleta Eugenia, the road is gradually advancing southeast

to **Puerto Toro,** where some 60 boats employ about four persons each in search of *centolla* (king crab).

## Cordón de los Dientes

Immediately south of Puerto Williams, Cordón de los Dientes is a range of jagged peaks rising more than 1,000 meters above sea level that offers the world's southernmost trekking opportunities. There are, however, few trails through this rugged countryside—anyone undertaking the four- to five-day "circuit" should be experienced in route finding.

## PORVENIR

Chilean Tierra del Fuego's main town, Porvenir sits on a sheltered harbor on the east side of the Strait of Magellan. Local settlement dates from the 1880s, when the area experienced a brief gold rush, but stabilized with the establishment of wool *estancias* around the turn of the century. After the wool boom fizzled in the 1920s, it settled into an economic torpor that, appropriately enough, has left it a remarkable assortment of corroding metal-clad Magellanic buildings. The construction of a salmon-processing plant has jump-started the local economy, and it's a much more presentable place than in the recent past.

Porvenir's inner harbor is a great place for spotting kelp geese, gulls, cormorants, steamer ducks, and other seabirds, but the lack of public transportation to the Argentine border has marginalized the town's tourist sector—all buses from the mainland to Argentine Tierra del Fuego take the longer Primera Angostura route, which involves a shorter and more frequent ferry crossing. Small local enterprises have begun to provide access to parts of the archipelago that, up to now, have only been accessible through expensive cruises.

Only 30 nautical miles east of Punta Arenas, Porvenir (pop. 4,734) occupies a protected site at the east end of Bahía Porvenir, an inlet of the Strait of Magellan. Its port, though, is three kilometers west of the town proper.

From Porvenir Ruta 215, a smooth gravel

© WAYNE BERNHARDSON

wool truck at Porvenir ferry dock, Chilean Tierra del Fuego

road, leads south and then east along the shore of Bahía Inútil to the Argentine border at San Sebastián, 150 kilometers away; an interesting alternate route leads directly east through the Cordón Baquedano before rejoining Ruta 215 about 55 kilometers to the east. If it's too late to catch the ferry back to Punta Arenas, another gravel road follows the coast to Puerto Espora, 141 kilometers to the northeast.

## Sights

Directly on the water, **Parque Yugoslavo** is a memorial to the earliest gold-seeking immigrants, most of whom were Croatians; it's also one of Porvenir's best bird-watching spots. The tourist office provides a small map/brochure, in English, of the city's distinctive architectural heritage; many of its houses, and other buildings, were also Croatian-built.

Most public buildings surround the neatly landscaped **Plaza de Armas,** two blocks north of Parque Yugoslavo. Among them is the expanded and improved **Museo de Tierra del Fuego Fernando Rusque Cordero** (Zavattaro 402, tel. 061/581800), a regional museum that deals with the island's natural history, indigenous heritage, the early gold rush, the later but longer-lasting wool rush, and even cinematography—German-born local filmmaker José Bohr actually went to Hollywood in 1929 and enjoyed a long if inconsistent career. It has added a skillfully done replica of an early rural store, and a good photographic display on local architecture.

The museum takes its name from a Carabineros officer who helped found it—and was no doubt responsible for the permanent exhibit on police uniforms. Weekday hours are 9 A.M.–5 P.M., while weekend hours are 10:30 A.M.–1:30 P.M. and 3–5 P.M. Admission costs US$1.

## Accommodations and Food

The no-frills **Hostal los Canelos** (Croacia 356, tel. 061/581223, US$11 pp) occupies a distinctive Magellanic house. There's no sign outside homey **Hospedaje Shinká** (Santos Mardones 333, tel. 061/580491, US$19/26 pp), but it offers better facilities and amenities—immaculate midsize rooms with comfortable beds, private bath, and cable TV—for less money than any other place in town. The breakfast is forgettable, but that's a minor fault for a place this good.

All rooms now have private bath at upgraded and expanded **Hotel España** (Croacia 698, tel. 061/580160, US$16 pp–US$23/41 s/d), whose utilitarian addition masks large new rooms; the cheapest rooms, in the older section, are smaller but still adequate. It also has a restaurant.

**Hostería Los Flamencos** (Teniente Merino s/n, tel. 061/580049, www.hosterialos flamencos.com, US$22/35 s/d) has undergone

a recent rehab, including much-needed interior and exterior paint, but kept prices reasonable.

In a lovingly restored Magellanic house with more character than any other accommodations in town, **Hostería Yendegaia** (Croacia 702, tel. 061/581665, www.turismo yendegaia.com, US$28/37 s/d) has spacious rooms in their original configuration, with high ceilings and contemporary comforts. It also has an appealing restaurant open to the public.

All rooms at **Hotel Rosas** (Philippi 269, tel. 02901/580088, US$30/40 s/d) have private bath and include breakfast; its restaurant is one of Porvenir's better values in a town with, admittedly, only a few options.

Other than hotel restaurants, the main dining

---

## TRAVEL IN CHILE

Many visitors to Argentine Patagonia also cross the border into Chilean Patagonia and Tierra del Fuego. In fact, anyone traveling overland to Argentine Tierra del Fuego *must* pass through Chile, though air passengers can avoid Argentina's smaller neighbor. Not that they would necessarily want to, as there's plenty to see and do there.

Because so many travelers to Patagonia visit bordering Magallanes and the Chilean side of Tierra del Fuego, key destinations like Punta Arenas, Parque Nacional Torres del Paine, and Puerto Williams are covered in detail in this book. For details on the rest of the country, see *Moon Chile*.

### VISAS AND OFFICIALDOM

Very few nationalities need advance visas, but requirements can change – if in doubt, check Chilean consulates in Río Gallegos, Río Grande, or Ushuaia. Ordinarily, border officials grant foreign tourists an automatic 90-day entry permit, but if arriving by air some nationalities must pay a so-called reciprocity fee, equivalent to what their own countries charge Chileans for a visa application.

In the case of U.S. citizens, for instance, it's US$100.

The paramilitary Carabineros serve as both immigration and customs officials at some Patagonian crossings; at the larger ones, most notably San Sebastián (Tierra del Fuego) and Monte Aymond (south of Río Gallegos), the Policía Internacional (International Police), the Servicio Nacional de Aduanas (National Customs Service), and the Servicio Agrícola y Ganadero (SAG, Agriculture and Livestock Service) have separate presences. Fresh fruit is the biggest taboo.

### HEALTH

Chile requires no vaccinations for visitors entering from any country, and public health standards are high. Generally, tap water is safe to drink, but short-term visitors should be cautious. As in Argentina, both Chagas' disease and hantavirus are present, but health risks in Patagonia and Tierra del Fuego are small indeed.

### MONEY AND PRICES

Until the Argentine economic meltdown of

options include the basic **Puerto Montt** (Croacia 1199, tel. 061/580207) and the **Club Social Catef** (Zavattaro 94, tel. 061/581399). **El Chispa** (Señoret 202, tel. 061/580054) is a *picada* with good home cooking at moderate prices.

At Bahía Chilote, **La Picá de Pechuga** (tel. 099/8886380) is a moderately priced seafood *picada* that gets its variety of fish fresh off the boat. The waterfront **Club Social Croata** (Señoret 542, tel. 061/580053) is more formal, but has good fish and wine by the glass, though the service can be erratic.

## Information and Services

In the same offices as the museum, Porvenir's steadily improving **Oficina Municipal de Turismo** (Padre Mario Zavattaro 434, tel. 061/581800, muniporvenir@terra.cl) keeps the same hours as the museum: 9 A.M.–5 P.M. weekdays, and 10:30 A.M.–1:30 P.M. and 3–5 P.M. weekends.

**Banco del Estado** (Philippi 263) has an ATM.

**Correos de Chile** (Philippi 176) is at the southwest corner of the Plaza de Armas. Alsmost alongside the bank, the **Centro de Llamados** (Philippi 277) has long-distance telephones.

For medical services, try the **Hospital Porvenir** (Carlos Wood s/n, between Señoret and Guerrero, tel. 061/580034).

## Getting There and Around

Porvenir has regular but infrequent connections

---

early 2002, Chile had been relatively inexpensive compared with its larger neighbor, but Argentina's devaluation reversed this relationship. It was not that Chilean prices increased significantly, but rather that Argentine prices dropped so precipitously that Chile became relatively more expensive. Since 2003, a steady revaluation of the Chilean peso against the U.S. dollar has made Chile increasingly costly.

Nevertheless, Chile has maintained economic stability and a low-inflation economy for at least a decade and a half. Travelers should keep a close eye on exchange rates, however.

Travelers checks are relatively easy to cash, but ATM cards are more convenient. A small reserve of cash in dollars is also a good idea.

One economic advantage of travel in Chile is that midrange to upscale hotels deduct IVA (value added tax) for foreign tourists who pay in U.S. dollars or by credit card. This means, for instance, that a US$100 hotel becomes a US$80 hotel, but it's not automatic – you must ask for it. The very cheapest accommodations, which are usually IVA-exempt, rarely follow this practice.

### SCHEDULES AND HOURS

Chileans, in general, rise later than Argentines, many businesses do not open until 10 A.M., and it's often difficult to get breakfast in a Chilean hotel before 8 A.M. Lunch tends to be a bit later than in Argentina, around 2 P.M., but dinner is as early as 8 P.M.

### COMMUNICATIONS

Telephone, Internet, and postal services are all moderately priced. Chile's country code is 56; the area code for Magallanes and Chilean Tierra del Fuego is 061. Prefixes for cell phones in the entire country are 098 and 099.

### GETTING AROUND

Distances in Chilean Patagonia are shorter than in Argentina, and the main highways are excellent. On the Chilean side of Tierra del Fuego, some roads are paved but most are gravel or dirt.

Chilean buses mostly resemble those in Argentina – modern, spacious, and fast. Neither Punta Arenas nor Puerto Natales, Magallanes's two main cities, has a central terminal. Prices resemble those in Argentina.

Plaza de Armas, Porvenir

to the mainland but none to the San Sebastián border crossing into Argentina; those with their own vehicles (including bicyclists) will still find this a shorter route from Punta Arenas to Ushuaia.

**Aerovías DAP** (Manuel Señoret s/n and Muñoz Gamero, tel. 061/580089) operates air taxi service to Punta Arenas (US$31) at least daily, often more frequently.

Tuesday and Friday at 4 P.M., there's a municipal bus from the DAP offices on Señoret to Camerón and Timaukel (US$2, 2.5 hours), in the southwestern corner of the island; another goes to **Cerro Sombrero** (US$4.50, 1.5 hours) at 5 P.M. Monday, Wednesday, and Friday from Zavattaro 432.

In the same office as DAP, **Transbordadora Broom** (Manuel Señoret s/n, tel. 061/580089) sails the car-passenger ferry *Melinka* to Punta Arenas (2.5 hours) daily except Monday, seas permitting. The ferry leaves from Bahía Chilote, about three kilometers west of town. Adult passengers pay US$7 per person except for the drivers, whose own fare is included in the US$45 charge per vehicle (motorcycles pay US$14). Children cost US$3.50 each.

## VICINITY OF PORVENIR

Vicinity is a relative term on Tierra del Fuego, as some fascinating locales are exceptionally difficult or expensive—or both—to reach. **Cordillera Darwin, Ltda.** (Croacia 675, tel. 061/50167 or 09/6407204, www.explore patagonia.cl) does brief dolphin-watching tours around Bahía Chilote, vehicle tours of the Cordón Baquedano, three-day horseback excursions to the Río Cóndor, and a six-day trip to the Cordillera Darwin that's substantially cheaper than the only other option, the luxury cruises on the *Mare Australis* and *Via Australis*.

### Monumento Natural Laguna de los Cisnes

International bird-watching groups often make a detour to this 25-hectare saline lake reserve, which sometimes dries out, just north of Porvenir. While it takes its name from the elegant black-necked swan, it is also home to many other species.

## Cordón Baquedano

After Chilean naval officer Ramón Serrano Montaner found gold in the rolling hills east of Porvenir in 1879, panners from Chile and Croatia flocked to the Río del Oro Valley, between the Cordón Baquedano and the Sierra Boquerón. Living in sod huts that shielded them from the wind and cold, hoping to eke out a kilogram per year—though yields were usually smaller—more than 200 worked the placers until they gave out. By the turn of the century, California miners introduced dredges and steam shovels, but decreasing yields ended the rush by 1908–1909. A few hardy individuals hang on even today.

From Porvenir, the eastbound road through the Cordón Baquedano passes several gold-rush sites, some marked with interpretive panels; the literal high point is the **Mirador de la Isla,** an overlook 500 meters above sea level. In many places guanacos, which seem to outnumber sheep, gracefully vault meter-high fences that stop the sheep cold.

## Onaisín

About 100 kilometers east of Porvenir, a major north–south road crosses Ruta 215 at Onaisín, a former Sociedad Explotadora *estancia* whose **Cementerio Inglés** is a national historical monument. Northbound, the road goes to the petroleum company town of Cerro Sombrero, while southbound it goes to Camerón and Lago Blanco.

## Lago Blanco

Some 50 kilometers southwest of Onaisín, the road passes through **Camerón,** an erstwhile picture-postcard *estancia* that is now a municipality, then angles southeast to Lago Blanco, an area known for its fishing and, until recently, a speculative and controversial project for native forest exploitation by the U.S.-based Trillium Corporation. In summer, there's a bumpy border crossing to Río Grande, Argentina, via a dirt road, with many livestock gates and a ford of the Río Rasmussen. The Argentine border post is called Radman.

On Isla Victoria, in the middle of Lago Blanco, **Lodge de Pesca Isla Victoria** (tel. 061/243354, US$144/174 s/d) caters to fly-fishermen.

## Estancia Yendegaia

Visited primarily by Chilean cruise ships and private yachts, Estancia Yendegaia conserves 44,000 hectares of native Fuegian forest in the Cordillera Darwin between the Argentine border and Parque Nacional Alberto de Agostini. While the owners hope to establish a private national park and create an unbroken preservation corridor along the Beagle Channel (Yendegaia borders Argentina's Parque Nacional Tierra del Fuego), there is government pressure to pave the *estancia's* airstrip at Caleta María, at the north end of the property, and a road south from Lago Blanco is already under construction. The owners, for their part, would

Estancia Yendegaia and Cordillera Darwin, Chilean Tierra del Fuego

© WAYNE BERNHARDSON

rather see the border opened to foot traffic from Argentina, but they have consulted with public-works officials to minimize the road's environmental impact.

In the meantime, the *estancia* is open to visitors—though access is difficult without chartering a plane or boat, or taking an expensive tour like the *Mare Australis* cruise through the Fuegian fjords; even this stops only on occasion. Naval boats between Punta Arenas and Puerto Williams may drop passengers here, but are so infrequent that getting back could be a problem. At some point, there should be accommodations available.

## CERRO SOMBRERO

About 70 kilometers north of Onaisín and 43 kilometers south of the Puerto Espora ferry landing, Cerro Sombrero is a company town where employees of Chile's Empresa Nacional de Petróleo (ENAP, National Petroleum Company) reside in orderly surroundings with remarkable amenities for a town with only about 150 houses. Dating from the early 1960s, it boasts an astronomical observatory, a bank, a botanical garden, a cinema, a hospital, recreational facilities including a heated swimming pool, and restaurants. Buses between Río Grande and Punta Arenas take a meal break at **Restaurant El Conti,** just outside town.

Overnighters will find accommodations at vastly improved **Hostería Tunkelén** (Arturo Prat 101, tel. 061/345001, US$53/71 s/d), which also has a new and very good (but rather expensive) restaurant.

# Punta Arenas

Patagonia's largest city, Punta Arenas is also the regional capital and the traditional port of entry, whether by sea, land, or air. Stretching north–south along the Strait of Magellan, the city boasts an architectural heritage that ranges from the Magellanic vernacular of metal-clad houses with steeply pitched roofs to elaborate Francophile mansions commissioned by 19th-century wool barons. Home to several museums, it's a good base for excursions to historical sites and nearby penguin colonies.

Punta Arenas's diverse economy depends on fishing, shipping, petroleum, duty-free retail, and tourism. Historically, it's one of the main gateways to Antarctica for both research and tourism, but in recent years the Argentine port of Ushuaia has absorbed much of this traffic. Ironically, in a region that grazes millions of sheep, it's hard to find woolens here because of the influx of artificial fabrics through the duty-free Zona Franca.

## HISTORY

After the collapse of Chile's initial Patagonian settlement at Fuerte Bulnes, Governor José Santos Mardones relocated northward to a site on the western shore of the Strait of Magellan, long known to British seamen as "Sandy Point." Soon expanded to include a penal colony, the town adopted that name in Spanish translation.

The Chileans' timing was propitious, as California's 1849 gold rush spurred a surge of shipping through the strait that helped keep the new city afloat—even if supplying sealskins, coal, firewood, and lumber did not exactly portend prosperity. A mutiny that resulted in Governor Benjamín Muñoz Gamero's death did little to improve matters, and traffic fell off in the following years.

What did bring prosperity was Governor Diego Dublé Almeyda's introduction of breeding sheep from the Falkland Islands. Their proliferation on the Patagonian plains, along with a vigorous immigration policy that brought entrepreneurs such as the Portuguese José Nogueira, the Spaniard José Menéndez, and the Irishman Thomas Fenton—not to mention the polyglot laborers who made their fortunes possible—helped transform the city from a dreary presidio to the booming port of a pastoral empire. Its mansions matched many in Buenos Aires, though the maldistribution of wealth and political power remained an intractable issue well into the 20th century.

As the wool economy declined around the end of World War II, petroleum discoveries on Tierra del Fuego and commercial fishing sustained the economy. Creation of Zona Franca duty-free areas gave commercial advantages to both Punta Arenas and the northern city of Iquique in the 1970s, and the tourist trade has flourished since the Pinochet dictatorship ended in 1989.

Punta Arenas (pop. about 116,105) is 210 kilometers southwest of Río Gallegos via the Argentine RN 3 and the Chilean Ruta 255 and Ruta 9; it is 241 kilometers southeast of Puerto Natales via Ruta 9. A daily vehicle ferry connects Punta with Porvenir, while a gravel road, the most southerly on the continent, leads to Fuerte Bulnes and Cabo San Isidro.

## SIGHTS

For a panoramic overview of the city's layout, the Strait of Magellan, and the island of Tierra del Fuego in the distance, climb to **Mirador La Cruz,** four blocks west of Plaza Muñoz Gamero via a staircase at the corner of Fagnano and Señoret.

### Plaza Muñoz Gamero and Vicinity

Unlike plazas founded in colonial Chilean cities, Punta Arenas's central plaza was not at first the focus of civic life, but thanks to European immigration and wealth generated by mining, livestock, commerce, and fishing, it became so by the 1880s. Landscaped with Monterey cypress and other exotic conifers, the plaza and surrounding buildings constitute a *zona típica* national monument; the plaza proper underwent a major renovation in 2004.

The plaza takes its name from early provincial governor Benjamín Muñoz Gamero, who died in an 1851 mutiny. Among its features are the Victorian kiosk (1910) that now houses the municipal tourist office and sculptor Guillermo Córdova's elaborate monument sponsored by wool magnate José Menéndez on the 400th

anniversary of Magellan's 1520 voyage. Magellan's imposing figure, embellished with a globe and a copy of his log, stand above a Selkn'am Indian representing Tierra del Fuego, a Tehuelche symbolizing Patagonia, and a mermaid with Chilean and regional coats of arms. According to local legend, anyone touching the Tehuelche's now well-worn toe—enough have done so to change its color—will return to Punta Arenas.

After about 1880, the city's burgeoning elite began to build monuments to their own good fortune, such as the ornate **Palacio Sara Braun** (1895), a national monument in its own right, at the plaza's northwest corner. Only six years after marrying the Portuguese José Nogueira, Punta's most prominent businessman, the newly widowed Sara Braun contracted French architect Numa Mayer, who applied contemporary Parisian style in designing a two-story

headstone of the wool baron José Menéndez, Cementerio Municipal, Punta Arenas, Chile

mansard building that contrasted dramatically with the city's earlier utilitarian architecture. Now home to the Club de la Unión and Hotel José Nogueira, the building retains most of its original features, including the west-facing winter garden that now serves as the hotel's bar/restaurant.

Mid-block, immediately east, the **Casa José Menéndez** belonged to another of Punta's wool barons, while at the plaza's northeast corner, the Comapa travel agency now occupies the former headquarters of the influential **Sociedad Menéndez Behety** (Magallanes 990). Half a block north, dating from 1904, the **Casa Braun-Menéndez** (Magallanes 949) houses the regional museum.

At the plaza's southwest corner, Punta Arenas's **Iglesia Matriz** (1901) now enjoys cathedral status. Immediately to its north, both the **Residencia del Gobernador** (Governors' Residence) and the **Gobernación** date from the same period, filling the rest of the block with offices of the Intendencia Regional, the regional government. On the south side, directly opposite the Victorian tourist kiosk, the former **Palacio Montes** now holds municipal government offices; at the southeast corner, the **Sociedad Braun Blanchard** belonged to another powerful commercial group (as should be obvious from the names, Punta Arenas's first families were, commercially at least, an incestuous bunch).

## Ⓒ Casa Braun-Menéndez (Museo Regional de Magallanes)

Like European royalty, Punta's first families formed alliances sealed by matrimony, and the Casa Braun-Menéndez (1904) is a classic example: the product of a marriage between Mauricio Braun (Sara's brother) and Josefina Menéndez Behety (daughter of José Menéndez and María Behety, a major wool-growing family in Argentina—though international borders meant little to wool barons).

Still furnished with the family's belongings, preserving Mauricio Braun's office and other rooms virtually intact, the house boasts marble fireplaces and other elaborate architectural

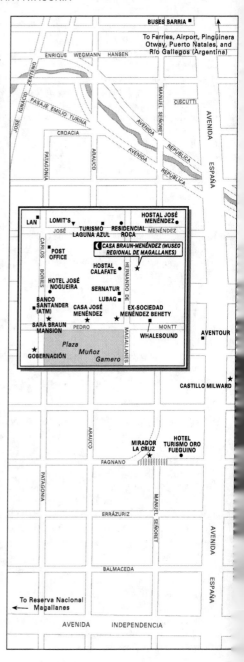

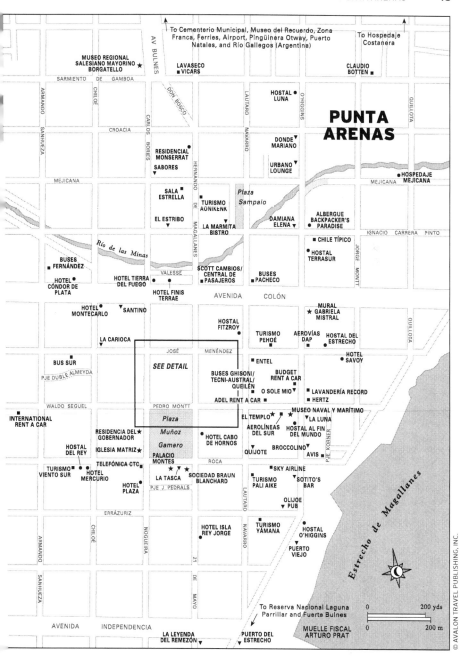

To Cementerio Municipal, Museo del Recuerdo, Zona Franca, Ferries, Airport, Pingüinera Otway, Puerto Natales, and Río Gallegos (Argentina)

To Hospedaje Costanera

**PUNTA ARENAS**

AV BULNES
ARMANDO
SANHUEZA
CHILOÉ
CARLOS BORIES
DON BOSCO
HERNANDO DE MAGALLANES
LAUTARO
NAVARRO
O'HIGGINS
QUILLOTA
JORGE MONTT
QUILLOTA
NOGUEIRA
21 DE MAYO
LAUTARO
NAVARRO

SARMIENTO DE GAMBOA
CROACIA
MEJICANA
IGNACIO CARRERA PINTO
MEJICANA
JOSÉ
MENÉNDEZ
PEDRO MONTT
ROCA
PJE J PEDRALS
ERRÁZURIZ
WALDO SEGUEL
PJE DUBLE ALMEYDA
AVENIDA COLÓN
AVENIDA INDEPENDENCIA

MUSEO REGIONAL SALESIANO MAYORINO BORGATELLO ★

LAVASECO ■ VICARS

CLAUDIO BOTTEN ■

HOSTAL ● LUNA

DONDE ▼ MARIANO

URBANO ▼ LOUNGE

HOSPEDAJE MEJICANA ●

RESIDENCIAL ● MONSERRAT
SABORES ■

SALA ■ ESTRELLA
■ TURISMO AÓNIKENK
EL ESTRIBO ▼
▼ LA MARMITA BISTRO ●

Plaza Sampaio

DAMIANA ELENA ▼

ALBERGUE BACKPACKER'S ● PARADISE

■ CHILE TÍPICO

● HOSTAL TERRASUR

BUSES ■ FERNÁNDEZ

Río de las Minas

HOTEL ● CÓNDOR DE PLATA

HOTEL TIERRA ■ DEL FUEGO

VALESSE

HOTEL FINIS TERRAE ●

SCOTT CAMBIOS/ CENTRAL DE ■ PASAJEROS

BUSES ■ PACHECO

MURAL ★ GABRIELA MISTRAL

HOTEL ● MONTECARLO
▼ SANTINO

HOSTAL FITZROY ■

TURISMO PEHOÉ ■

AERÓVIAS DAP ■

HOSTAL DEL ● ESTRECHO ■

HOTEL ● SAVOY

LA CARIOCA ▼

BUS SUR ■

■ ENTEL

SEE DETAIL

BUSES GHISONI/ TECNI-AUSTRAL/ QUEILÉN ■

BUDGET RENT A CAR ■

O SOLE MIO ▼ ■

■ LAVANDERÍA RECORD

ADEL RENT A CAR ■

■ HERTZ

INTERNATIONAL RENT A CAR ■

Plaza Muñoz Gamero

EL TEMPLO ★ ▼

▼ LA LUNA

■ MUSEO NAVAL Y MARÍTIMO

RESIDENCIA DEL ★ GOBERNADOR
IGLESIA MATRIZ ★

AEROLÍNEAS DEL SUR ▼

HOSTAL AL FIN ● DEL MUNDO

HOSTAL DEL REY ■

HOTEL ● CABO DE HORNOS

QUIJOTE ▼

BROCCOLINO ▼

AVIS ■

PJE EL KÖRNER

TELEFÓNICA CTC ■

TURISMO ■ VIENTO SUR
HOTEL ● MERCURIO

LA TASCA ■

SOCIEDAD BRAUN BLANCHARD ■

■ SKY AIRLINE

HOTEL ● PLAZA

PALACIO MONTES ★ ★ ▼ ★

TURISMO PALI AIKE ■

▼ SOTITO'S BAR

OLIJOE ▼ PUB

HOTEL ISLA ● REY JORGE ■

TURISMO ■ YÁMANA ▼

HOSTAL ● O'HIGGINS

▼ PUERTO VIEJO

Estrecho de Magallanes

To Reserva Nacional Laguna Parrillar and Fuerte Bulnes

LA LEYENDA ■ DEL REMEZÓN ▼

PUERTO DEL ■ ESTRECHO ▼

MUELLE FISCAL ARTURO PRAT

| 0 | | 200 yds |
| 0 | | 200 m |

features. The basement servants' quarters reveal the classic upstairs-downstairs division of early-20th-century society.

Today, the Casa Braun-Menéndez (Magallanes 949, tel. 061/244216, museomag@ entelchile.net) serves as the regional museum, replete with pioneer settlers' artifacts and historical photographs. There are imperfect but readable English descriptions of the exhibits. On some days, a pianist plays beneath the atrium's stained-glass skylight.

November–April, the Casa Braun-Menéndez is open 10 A.M.–5 P.M. daily except for major holidays; the rest of the year, it closes at 2 P.M. Admission costs US$2 for adults, US$1 for children.

## Museo Regional Salesiano Mayorino Borgatello

From the 19th century, the Salesian order played a key role in evangelizing southern Patagonia and Tierra del Fuego, in both Chile and Argentina. Punta Arenas was their base and, while their rosy view of Christianity's impact on the region's native people may be debatable, figures such as the Italian mountaineer priest Alberto de Agostini (1883–1960) made major contributions to both physical geography and ethnographic understanding of the region.

Agostini left a sizeable collection of photographs, both ethnographic and geographical, preserved in the museum, which also has a library and a small regionally oriented art gallery. Permanent exhibits deal with regional flora and fauna, a handful of early colonial artifacts, regional ethnography, the missionization of Isla Dawson and other nearby areas, cartography, and the petroleum industry. For Darwinians, there's a scale model of the *Beagle* and, for Chilean patriots, one of the *Ancud,* which sailed from Chiloé to claim the region in 1843.

The Museo Regional Salesiano (Avenida Bulnes 336, tel. 061/221001, musborga@tnet. cl) is open 10 A.M.–6 P.M. daily except Monday. Admission costs US$3.50 for adults, US$0.35 for children.

## Museo Naval y Marítimo

Pleasantly surprising, Punta Arenas's naval and maritime museum provides perspectives on topics like ethnography—in the context of the Strait of Magellan's seagoing indigenous peoples—even while stressing its military mission. It features interactive exhibits, such as a credible warship's bridge, a selection of model ships, and information on the naval history of the southern oceans.

The most riveting material, though, concerns Chilean pilot Luis Pardo Villalón's 1916 rescue of British explorer Ernest Shackleton's crew at Elephant Island, on the Antarctic peninsula. On the cutter *Yelcho,* with neither heat, electricity, nor radio in foggy and stormy winter weather, Pardo returned the entire crew to Punta Arenas in short order; he later served as Chilean consul in Liverpool.

The Museo Naval (Pedro Montt 981, tel. 061/205479, terzona@armada.cl) is open 9:30 A.M.–12:30 P.M. and 3–5 P.M. daily except Sunday and Monday. Admission costs US$2 for adults, US$0.60 for children.

## Museo del Recuerdo

Run by the Instituto de la Patagonia, itself part of the Universidad de Magallanes, the Museo del Recuerdo is a mostly open-air facility displaying pioneer agricultural implements and industrial machinery, reconstructions of a traditional house and shearing shed, and a restored shepherd's trailer house (hauled across the Patagonian plains on wooden wheels). In addition to a modest botanical garden, the Instituto itself has a library/bookshop with impressive cartographic exhibits.

Admission to the Museo del Recuerdo (Avenida Bulnes 01890, tel. 061/207056) costs US$2 for adults, free for children. Hours are 8:30 A.M.–11 P.M. and 2:30–6 P.M. weekdays. From downtown Punta Arenas, taxi *colectivos* to the Zona Franca (duty-free zone) stop directly opposite the entrance.

## Other Sights

Four blocks south of Plaza Muñoz Gamero,

at the foot of Avenida Independencia, naval vessels, freighters, cruise ships, Antarctic icebreakers, and yachts from many countries dock at the **Muelle Fiscal Arturo Prat,** the city's major port facility until recently. It's still a departure point for cruises to the fjords of Tierra del Fuego and to Antarctica but, unfortunately, international security issues have meant closing it to spontaneous public access.

The late, gifted travel writer Bruce Chatwin found the inspiration for his legendary vignettes of *In Patagonia* through tales of his eccentric distant relative Charley Milward, who built and resided at the **Castillo Milward** (Milward's Castle, Avenida España 959). Described by Chatwin as "a Victorian parsonage translated to the Strait of Magellan," with "high-pitched gables and gothic windows," the building features a square tower street-side and an octagonal one at the back.

At the corner of Avenida Colón and O'Higgins, gracing the walls of the former **Liceo de Niñas Sara Braun** (Sara Braun Girls School), rises a weathering seven-meter **Mural Gabriela Mistral,** honoring the Nobel Prize poetess.

Ten blocks north of Plaza Muñoz Gamero, the **Cementerio Municipal** (Avenida Bulnes 029) is home to the extravagant crypts of José Menéndez, José Nogueira, and Sara Braun, but the multinational immigrants who worked for them—English, Scots, Welsh, Croat, German, and Scandinavian—repose in more modest circumstances. A separate monument honors the vanished Selkn'am (Ona) Indians who once flourished in the strait, while another memorializes German fatalities of the Battle of the Falklands (1914).

## ENTERTAINMENT

Except on Sunday, when the city seems as dead as the cemetery, there's usually something to do.

Punta Arenas has one surviving cinema, the **Sala Estrella** (Mejicana 777, tel. 061/241262).

**El Templo** (Pedro Montt 951, tel.

061/223667) is primarily a dance club. The stylish **Olijoe Pub** (Errázuriz 970) has the feel of an upscale English pub, with paneled walls, ceiling, and bar, and reasonably priced drinks; the music, though, can get a little loud for conversation. The Sara Braun mansion's basement **Taberna Club de la Unión** (Plaza Muñoz Gamero 716, tel. 061/617133) is exceptionally popular on weekends.

**Santino** (Avenida Colón 657, tel. 061/710882, www.santino.cl) is a spacious and informal pub where everyone feels welcome; there's also food, but it's not the star. With its techno ambience, **Urbano Lounge** (O'Higgins 568, tel. 061/224044) has a self-consciously exclusive, even pretentious feel; again, the food plays second fiddle to the bar.

At the north end of town, **Makanudo** (El Ovejero 474, tel. 09/6492031) has 7–10 P.M. happy hours weekdays except Friday, and live music Friday and Saturday nights from around 1:30 A.M.

The **Club Hípico** (municipal racetrack) fronts on Avenida Bulnes between Coronel Mardones and Manantiales, north of downtown. Professional soccer matches take place at the **Estadio Fiscal,** a few blocks north at Avenida Bulnes and José González.

## SHOPPING

Though it's faltered in recent years, Punta Arenas's major shopping destination is the duty-free Zona Franca, four kilometers north of downtown but easily reached by *taxi colectivo* from Calle Magallanes. Traditionally, consumer electronics were the big attraction—Santiaguinos even flew here for the bargains—but price differentials are smaller than they used to be.

**Puerto del Estrecho** (O'Higgins 1401, tel. 061/241022) is a good if fairly pricey souvenir shop; in addition, it has an upstairs café, Internet access, and long-distance telephone service.

For crafts such as metal (copper and bronze), semi-precious stones (lapis lazuli), and woolens, visit **Chile Típico** (Ignacio Carrera Pinto 1015, tel. 061/225827). For books (including some local guidebooks and travel literature in English), maps, and keepsakes, try **Southern Patagonia Souvenirs & Books;** since its Bories location burned down, it has outlets at the airport (tel. 061/211591) and at the Zona Franca (tel. 061/216759).

## ACCOMMODATIONS
Sernatur maintains a complete list of accommodations with up-to-date prices. What in many other parts of Chile would be called *residenciales* are *hostales* (B&Bs) here. Some relatively expensive places have cheaper rooms with shared bath that can be excellent values.

### US$10-25
With the Chilean peso's steady appreciation, finding truly shoestring accommodations has become difficult, but some options remain. Under new ownership, the improved **Albergue Backpacker's Paradise** (Ignacio Carrera Pinto 1022, tel. 061/240104, backpackersparadise@hotmail.com, US$7 pp) is still a crowded hostel, but for the price it has its public. On the plus side, it has adequate common spaces with cable TV, cooking privileges, and Internet access.

Along the shoreline, east of the racetrack at the foot of Quillota, **Hospedaje Costanera** (Rómulo Correa 1221, tel. 061/240175, hospedajecostanera@hotmail.com, US$11 pp) has drawn favorable commentary. **Hospedaje Mejicana** (Mejicana 1174, tel. 061/227678, yoya_h@hotmail.com, US$9 pp, US$13/23 s/d) has also made good impressions.

### US$25-50
Often full, despite mixed reviews, **Hostal Dinka's House** (Caupolicán 169, tel./fax 061/244292, www.dinkaspatagonia.com, US$13 pp, US$19/26 s/d) has rooms with private and shared bath; the nearby annex is definitely substandard.

◖ **Hostal Fitz Roy** (Lautaro Navarro 850, tel./fax 061/240430, hostalfitzroy@hotmail.com, US$19/28 s/d with shared bath) is an old-fashioned bed-and-breakfast offering some modern comforts—notably cable TV and phones in each room—along with peace and quiet, and an excellent breakfast that includes fresh homemade bread and eggs. Returned to their original configuration, the rooms are spacious, but buildings of this vintage still have creaky floors and staircases. There are separate *cabañas* with private bath (US$46 d), and also ample parking.

In a distinctive Magellanic house, friendly, well-kept **Residencial Monserrat** (Magallanes 538, tel. 061/246661, www.residencial monserrat.cl, US$11 pp, US$24–31 s or d) has drawn praise from recent guests. Prices vary according to shared or private bath, and kitchen access is also available.

**Hostal del Rey** (Fagnano 589, Departamento B, tel./fax 061/223924, delrey@chileaustral.com, US$15 pp, US$33 d) is a friendly family place with only three doubles and two singles, so it's often full—call ahead. Rates include an ample breakfast, but the tobacco-laden air is a drawback. Some rooms now have private bath.

Only a block from the plaza, creaky **Residencial Roca** (Magallanes 888, 2nd floor, tel./fax 061/243903, franruiz@entelchile.net, US$11–17 pp) has rooms with either shared or private bath, cable TV, laundry service, and a book exchange.

**Hostal Luna** (O'Higgins 424, tel. 061/221764, hostalluna@hotmail.com, US$11–17 pp) has plain but well-furnished and even homey rooms—every bed has a cozy duvet—and provides a simple breakfast. The spacious dining room has cable TV, but the rooms do not.

In a large old house that's been subdivided, rooms at **Hostal al Fin del Mundo** (O'Higgins 1026, tel. 061/710185, alfindelmundo@123.cl, US$18 pp with shared bath) vary in size and quality, but it has its good points (including proximity to some of the city's best restaurants).

Near the old port, improved **Hostal O'Higgins** (O'Higgins 1205, tel. 061/227999, US$13 pp, US$37 d) has rooms with shared and private bath. Plain but clean and friendly, it also has ample secure parking.

Rehabbed and improved **Hotel Montecarlo** (Avenida Colón 605, tel. 061/222120, administracion@h-montecarlo.com, US$18/32–34/40 s/d) is once again worth consideration; the more expensive rooms have private bath.

## US$50-100

Prices have risen significantly at well-regarded, cul-de-sac **Hostal Sonia** (Pasaje Darwin 175, tel. 061/248543, www.hostalsk.50megs.com, US$37/53 s/d), which has rooms with private bath and breakfast.

Low-key **Hostal Terrasur** (O'Higgins 723, tel. 061/225618, www.hostalterrasur.cl, US$46/65 s/d) is one of the more appealing bed-and-breakfast-style places in its range. Rates include cable TV, telephone, and continental breakfast.

Though it's well-kept, rising prices make **Hostal José Menéndez** (José Menéndez 882, tel. 061/221279, www.chileaustral.com/jose menendez, US$33/46–46/65 s/d) a lesser value than it once was, especially since some rooms are small. Still, it's friendly, central, arranges tours, has parking, and offers a decent breakfast; rates vary according to shared or private bath.

Despite its misleadingly small street-side facade, **Hostal Calafate** (Magallanes 926, www.calafate.cl, tel./fax 061/241281, US$35/54–58/71 s/d) is a rambling building with spacious rooms that once held the former Hotel Oviedo; remodeled just a few years ago, it keeps a couple so-called *celdas de castigo* ("prison cells") for backpacker clients for US$15 per person—a pretty good deal in a well-kept, central facility. It also has some of Punta's best Internet facilities, also open to nonguests.

**Hotel Savoy** (José Menéndez 1073, tel./fax 061/247979, www.hotelsavoy.cl, US$56/72 s/d) lacks style—some interior walls have cheap plywood paneling—but the rooms are large and comfortable, and the staff is responsive.

◖ **Hostal Turismo Oro Fueguino** (Fagnano 356, tel. 061/249401, www.orofueguino.com, US$60/75 s/d) is still a good hotel, but the cheap aluminum siding and faux brick have destroyed its deco-style integrity. Rising rates include cable TV, telephone, central heating, breakfast, and private bath; some rooms are windowless but have skylights.

**Hotel Cóndor de Plata** (Avenida Colón 556, tel. 061/247987, fax 061/241149, US$60/75 s/d) has always been a good choice, but its prices are less competitive than they once were.

Half a block south of Plaza Muñoz Gamero, **Hotel Plaza** (Nogueira 1116, tel. 061/241300, fax 061/248613, www.chileaustral.com/hplaza, US$78/95 s/d) is a classic of the wool boom era.

Occupying a stylishly modernized building, **Hotel Mercurio** (Fagnano 595, tel./fax 061/242300, mercurio@chileaustral.com, US$76/97 s/d) offers both convenience and charm, with gracious staff to boot.

## Over US$100

Punta Arenas has a good selection of upscale, mostly modern or modernized hotels, such as the contemporary **Hotel Tierra del Fuego** (Avenida Colón 716, tel./fax 061/226200, www.puntaarenas.com, US$98/118 s/d), a business-oriented facility.

◖ **Hotel Isla Rey Jorge** (21 de Mayo 1243, tel. 061/222681, www.islareyjorge.com, US$119/146 s/d) is one of the best places to stay and town and a favorite with foreign tour groups. **Hotel Finis Terrae** (Avenida Colón 766, tel. 061/228200, www.hotelfinisterrae.com, US$154/176 d) is another fine newer hotel.

Punta Arenas's most distinctively historic accommodations, the ◖ **Hotel José Nogueira** (Bories 959, tel. 061/248840, www.hotel nogueira.com, US$149/179 s/d) occupies part of the Sara Braun mansion, known for its beautiful period architecture. Its greenhouse bar/restaurant, with its snaking grape arbor, merits a visit even if you can't afford to stay here.

Traditionally one of Punta's best, built by the Sociedad Ganadera Tierra del Fuego, the 1960s high-rise **Hotel Cabo de Hornos** (Plaza Muñoz Gamero 1025, tel. 061/715000, fax 061/229473, www.hotelcabodehornos.cl or www.hch.co.cl, US$180/200 s/d) has undergone not just a facelift but a full-scale makeover under new ownership.

## FOOD

Punta Arenas's fast-improving gastronomic scene ranges from fast food to haute cuisine.

With the appreciating Chilean peso, prices are increasing rapidly.

**Quijote** (Lautaro Navarro 1087, tel. 061/241225) serves inexpensive lunches. Upstairs in the Casa del Turista, at the entrance to Muelle Prat, **Café Puerto del Estrecho** (O'Higgins 1401, tel. 061/241022) has a variety of espresso-based specialty coffees, such as mocha and amaretto, plus snacks and desserts to accompany them.

Punta Arenas's best fast-food alternative is **◖ Lomit's** (José Menéndez 722, tel. 061/243399), a dependable sandwich-and-beer chain that's almost always packed. Sandwiches cost around US$5. **La Carioca** (José Menéndez 600, tel. 061/224809), by contrast, is a one-of-a-kind sandwich outlet that also serves passable pizza, pasta, and draft beer.

Despite a slight name change, **Dónde Mariano** (O'Higgins 504, tel. 061/245291) continues under the same management and delivers on its modest pretensions, serving fine if simply prepared fish entrées, including a side order, in the US$7–10 range. The decor has improved, and the service is adept.

On the former site of the landmark restaurant La Luna (and under the same management), **O Sole Mio** (O'Higgins 974, tel. 061/242026) serves a diversity of pastas with creative touches—spinach gnocchi, for instance—and excellent seafood sauces. Prices are moderate, around US$7 per entrée, and it's kept most of the old La Luna's informal atmosphere and decor, including classic (and newer) movie posters.

In a new location half a block south of its old haunts, **◖ La Luna** (O'Higgins 1017, tel. 061/228555) still buzzes with activity—pins stuck on wall maps indicate the origins of their clientele—but the transition seems to have cost it some of its informality. Even the *chupe de centolla* (king crab casserole, US$11) isn't quite what it was, but it's too early to write the place off.

Stick with the meat at **El Estribo** (Ignacio Carrera Pinto 762, tel. 061/244714); their fish is only so-so, but the beef and lamb dishes, in the US$7–12 and up range, are consistently

strong, and Patagonian game dishes have earned a spot on the menu. The English menu translation is occasionally hilarious, but the service is attentive.

Locals recommend the recently opened **La Marmita Bistro** (Plaza Sampaio 678, tel. 061/222056) for creative vegetarian plates and other specialties. For US$22, **Sabores** (Mejicana 702, 2nd floor, tel. 061/227369) serves a four-course "Magellanic menu" (US$22) that includes both king crab and salmon, as well as a pisco sour and half bottle of wine; Wednesdays are all-you-can-eat pasta nights (US$7 pp).

In the opinion of many, Punta's best is **◖ Damiana Elena** (O'Higgins 694, tel. 061/222818), where reservations are essential on weekends and advisable even on weeknights. Decorated with antiques, this restored period house serves beef and seafood specialties in the US$8–13 range—modest prices for the quality it offers—with unobtrusive service. There is limited tobacco-free seating, for which reservations are particularly advisable.

Another good choice is the nautically themed **◖ Puerto Viejo** (O'Higgins 1205, tel. 061/225103), doing bang-up business with an almost exclusively seafood menu. Open for lunch and dinner, with knowledgeable waiters and terrific service, it serves specialties such as *centolla* (king crab) and *merluza* (hake). On the down side, the pisco/*calafate* sours are mixed in advance, though they're still pretty fresh.

Under the same management, a couple kilometers north of the plaza, **◖ Los Ganaderos** (Avenida Bulnes 0977, tel. 061/214597, www.parrillalosganaderos.cl) is a classy *parrilla* specializing in succulent Patagonian lamb grilled on a vertical spit—for US$15 *tenedor libre* (all-you-can-eat) per person. There is also a more diverse *parrillada* for two (US$25), and pasta dishes in the US$8 range. Try the regional Patagonian desserts, such as *mousse de calafate* and *mousse de ruibarbo* (rhubarb).

Four blocks south of the plaza, the creative **◖ La Leyenda del Remezón** (21 de Mayo 1469, tel. 061/241029) serves game dishes (beaver and guanaco are now being farmed in the region) in the US$20 range—not cheap, obviously, but unique. Seafood specialties include krill, king crab, and spider crab.

Under a new concessionaire, in the old Centro Español, the upstairs **La Tasca** (Plaza Muñoz Gamero 771, tel. 061/242807) has been reborn as a cheerful midrange to upmarket Spanish restaurant with creative variants on traditional dishes, such as *merluza* (hake) stuffed with king crab and avocado (US$11). The pisco sours are excellent, and the wine list far better than it once was.

Promising ◖ **Brocolino** (O'Higgins 1049, tel. 061/710479) serves a fine risotto with *centolla* and scallops, along with beef, lamb, and pastas in the US$10–12 range. Traditionally, **Sotito's Bar** (O'Higgins 1138, tel. 061/245365) has set the seafood standard here, and it still deserves consideration.

## INFORMATION

A couple doors north of Plaza Muñoz Gamero, **Sernatur** (Magallanes 960, tel. 061/225385, infomagallanes@sernatur.cl) is open 8:15 A.M.– 6 P.M. weekdays. One of Chile's better regional offices, it has English-speaking personnel, up-to-date accommodations and transportation information, and a message board.

In summer, Plaza Muñoz Gamero's municipal **Kiosko de Informaciones** (tel. 061/200610, informacionturistica@puntaarenas.cl) is open 8 A.M.–8 P.M. weekdays, 9 A.M.–6 P.M. Saturday, and 9:30 A.M.–2:30 P.M. Sunday. It also has free Internet access for brief periods (longer if no one is waiting).

**Conaf** (Avenida Bulnes 0309, 4th floor, tel. 061/238581) provides information on the region's national parks.

## SERVICES

Punta Arenas is one of the easier Chilean cities in which to change both cash and travelers checks, especially at travel agencies along Lautaro Navarro. Most close by midday Saturday, but **Scott Cambios** (Avenida Colón and Magallanes, tel. 061/245811) will cash travelers checks then.

Several banks in the vicinity of Plaza Muñoz Gamero have ATMs, such as **Banco Santander** (Magallanes 997).

Just north of Plaza Muñoz Gamero, **Correos de Chile** (Bories 911) is the post office.

Long-distance call centers include **Telefónica CTC** (Nogueira 1116), at the southwest corner of Plaza Muñoz Gamero, and **Entel** (Lautaro Navarro 931). Try also **Hostal Calafate** (Magallanes 922), which has expanded its hotel business with an Internet café and phone center, now the best in town.

The **Argentine consulate** (21 de Mayo 1878, tel. 061/261912) is open 10 A.M.– 3:30 P.M. weekdays. Countries with honorary consulates include Brazil (Arauco 769, tel. 061/241093), Spain (José Menéndez 910, tel. 061/243566), and the United Kingdom (tel. 061/211535).

For clean clothes, try **Lavandería Record** (O'Higgins 969, tel. 061/243607) or **Lavaseco Vicars** (Sarmiento de Gamboa 726, tel. 061/241516).

Punta Arenas's **Hospital Regional** (Arauco and Angamos, tel. 061/244040) is north of downtown.

## GETTING THERE

Punta Arenas has good air connections to mainland Chile, frequent air service to Chilean Tierra del Fuego, infrequent flights to Argentine Tierra del Fuego, and regular weekly service to the Falkland Islands. There are roundabout overland routes to mainland Chile via Argentina, regular bus service to Argentine Tierra del Fuego via a ferry link, direct ferry service to Chilean Tierra del Fuego, and expensive (but extraordinarily scenic) cruise-ship service to Ushuaia, in Argentine Tierra del Fuego.

### Air

**LAN/LanExpress** (Bories 884, tel. 061/241232) flies four times daily to Santiago, normally via Puerto Montt, but some flights stop at Balmaceda, near Coyhaique. It also flies three times weekly to Ushuaia, Argentina, and Saturday to the Falkland Islands; one Falklands flight per month stops in the Argentine city of Río Gallegos.

**Sky Airline** (Roca 935, tel. 061/710645) now flies north to Balmaceda/Coyhaique, Puerto Montt, and Santiago, with connections to northern Chilean cities. **Aerolíneas del Sur** (Pedro Montt 969, tel. 061/221020) has similar routes.

**Aerovías DAP** (O'Higgins 891, tel. 061/223340, fax 061/221693, www.aerovias dap.cl) flies seven-seat Cessnas to and from Porvenir (US$23 plus taxes), in Chilean Tierra del Fuego, at least daily except Sunday, more often in summer. Daily except Sunday and Monday, it flies 20-seater Twin Otters to and from Puerto Williams on Isla Navarino (US$64 plus taxes). In addition, it has extensive charter services, and occasionally goes to Antarctica.

## Bus

Punta Arenas has no central terminal, though some companies share facilities and the **Central de Pasajeros** (Avenida Colón and Magallanes, tel. 061/245811) sells tickets for all of them. Most terminals are within a few blocks of each other, north of Plaza Muñoz Gamero. Services vary seasonally, with the greatest number of buses in January and February.

Several carriers serve Puerto Natales (US$5, three hours), including **Bus Sur** (José Menéndez 565, tel. 061/227145), with four buses daily; **Buses Fernández** (Armando Sanhueza 745, tel. 061/242313, www.busesfernandez .com, seven daily); **Buses Pacheco** (Avenida Colón 900, tel. 061/225527, three daily), and **Buses Transfer** (Pedro Montt 966, tel. 061/229613, one daily).

In addition to its Puerto Natales services, Buses Pacheco goes to the Chilean cities of Osorno (US$80, 28–30 hours), Puerto Montt, and Castro, Wednesday at 9 A.M., via Argentina. **Queilén Bus** (Lautaro Navarro 975, tel. 061/222714) and **Turibús** (Armando Sanhueza 745, tel. 061/227970) alternate services to Puerto Montt and Castro most mornings at 9:30 A.M. In addition to its Puerto Natales services, Bus Sur goes to Coyhaique (US$50, 20 hours) Monday at 10:30 A.M.

Several carriers go to Río Gallegos (US$10,

four hours): **Buses Pingüino** (Armando Sanhueza 745, tel. 061/221812 or 061/242313), **Buses Ghisoni** (Lautaro Navarro 975, tel. 061/710329), and Buses Pacheco (Avenida Colón 900, tel. 061/225527).

**Tecni-Austral** (Lautaro Navarro 975, tel. 061/222078) goes to Río Grande (US$22–25, eight hours) and Ushuaia (US$32, 11.5 hours), in Argentine Tierra del Fuego, Tuesday, Thursday, and Saturday at 8 A.M. **Bus Sur** goes Tuesday, Thursday, and Saturday at 9 A.M. to Río Grande, with connections to Ushuaia, while **Buses Barria** (Avenida España 264, tel. 061/240646) goes Wednesday and Saturday at 8 A.M.

Buses Barria connects directly to Parque Nacional Torres del Paine via Puerto Natales at 7 A.M. daily, at least in summer.

## Sea

**Transbordadora Austral Broom** (Avenida Bulnes 05075, tel. 061/218100, www.tabsa .cl) sails from Punta Arenas to Porvenir (2.5 hours) at 9 A.M. daily except Sunday, when sailing time is 9:30 A.M. Adult passengers pay US$7 per person except for the drivers, whose own fare is included in the US$45 charge per vehicle (motorcycles pay US$14). Children cost US$3.50 each. Given limited vehicle capacity, reservations are a good idea on the *Melinka,* which leaves from Terminal Tres Puentes, at the north end of town but easily accessible by taxi *colectivo* from the Casa Braun-Menéndez, on Magallanes half a block north of Plaza Muñoz Gamero.

Broom also operates the ferry *Cruz Australis* to Puerto Williams (32 hours) every Wednesday at 6 P.M., returning Friday at 10 P.M. The fare is US$150 for a bunk, US$120 for a reclining seat.

It's neither cheap nor a conventional way of getting to Argentina, but the luxury cruisers MV *Mare Australis* and MV *Via Australis* shuttle to Ushuaia as part of a week-long circuit through the fjords of Chilean Tierra del Fuego, and passengers can disembark in Ushuaia (or board there). Normally both ships require reservations well in advance.

## GETTING AROUND

Punta Arenas's **Aeropuerto Presidente Carlos Ibáñez del Campo** is 20 kilometers north of town on Ruta 9, the Puerto Natales highway. **Transfer al Aeropuerto** (Lautaro Navarro 975, tel. 061/222241) arranges door-to-door transfers for US$4 pp.

Buses returning from Puerto Natales will normally drop their passengers at the airport to meet outgoing flights on request, but make arrangements before boarding. Natales-bound buses will also pick up arriving passengers, but again make arrangements in advance.

Punta Arenas has numerous car-rental options, including **Adel Rent a Car** (Pedro Montt 962, tel. 061/235472, gerson@adentalrentacar.cl), **Budget** (O'Higgins 964, tel./fax 061/241696, budget@ctcinternet.cl), **Avis** (Roca 1044, tel./fax 061/241182, rentacar@viaterra.cl), **Hertz** (O'Higgins 987, tel. 061/248742, fax 061/244729), **International** (Waldo Seguel 443, tel. 061/228323, fax 061/226334, internationalrac@entelchile.net), and **Lubag** (Magallanes 970, tel./fax 061/242023, luis_barra@entelchile.net).

For rental bikes, contact **Claudio Botten** (Sarmiento de Gamboa 1132, tel. 061/242107 or 09/1684118, cbotten@ze.cl).

# Arenas

Punta Arenas's myriad travel agencies operate a variety of excursions to nearby destinations such as Reserva Nacional Magallanes, Fuerte Bulnes, the Seno Otway penguin colony, Río Verde, Estancia San Gregorio, and even Parque Nacional Torres del Paine. The most popular half-day excursions, such as Fuerte Bulnes and Otway, cost US$15–20 per person, while full-day trips such as Pali Aike can cost up to US$90 per person.

Among the established operators are **Aventour** (Avenida España 872, tel. 061/241197, www.aventourpatagonia.com), **Turismo Aónikenk** (Magallanes 619, tel. 061/221982, www.aonikenk.com), **Turismo Laguna Azul** (José Menéndez 786, tel. 061/225200, agencialagunaazul@yahoo.com), **Turismo Pali Aike** (Lautaro Navarro 1125, tel. 061/229388, www.turismopaliaike.com), **Turismo Viento Sur** (Fagnano 585, tel. 061/710840, www.vientosur.com), and **Turismo Yámana** (Errázuriz 932, tel. 061/710568, www.turismoyamana.cl).

## RESERVA NACIONAL MAGALLANES

Only eight kilometers west of downtown, 13,500-hectare Reserva Nacional Magallanes is a combination of Patagonian steppe and southern beech forest that, in good winters, amasses enough snow for skiing. Despite its proximity to Punta Arenas, official statistics say it gets barely 8,000 visitors per year, and fewer than 300 of those are foreigners.

From westbound Avenida Independencia, a good gravel road that may require chains in winter climbs gradually to a fork whose southern branch leads to the reserve's **Sector Andino,** where the local Club Andino's **Centro de Esquí Cerro Mirador** includes a *refugio* that serves meals, a ski school, and a single well-maintained chairlift. In summer, try the **Sendero Mirador,** a two-hour loop hike that winds through the forest and crosses the ski area; there's also a mountain-bike circuit.

The northwesterly **Sector Las Minas,** which includes a gated picnic area, charges US$2 per person for adult admission, but nothing for kids. A longer footpath links up with the trail to the El Mirador summit, which offers panoramas east toward Punta Arenas, the strait, and Tierra del Fuego, and west toward Seno Otway.

Though some Punta Arenas travel agencies offer tours to the reserve, it would also be a good mountain-bike excursion from town.

## PINGÜINERA SENO OTWAY

Burrowing Magellanic penguins abound along Argentine Patagonia's Atlantic shoreline, but they are fewer in Chile. Barely an hour from Punta Arenas, though, the *Spheniscus magellanicus* colony at Seno Otway (Otway Sound) is the closest to any major city on the continent. Under the administration of the non-profit Fundación Otway, it grew in a decade from no more than 400 penguins to about 8,000 breeding pairs at present. From October, when the first birds arrive, to April, when the last stragglers head to sea, it draws up to 40,000 visitors. The peak season, though, is December–February.

While the site is fenced to keep human visitors out of critical habitat, the birds are relatively tame and easy to photograph; on the down side, this did not prevent stray dogs from killing more than a hundred birds in 2001. The land-owning Kusanovic family has recently taken over management from the Fundación Otway.

During the season, any number of Punta Arenas operators shuttle visitors to and from the Otway site for about US$10–12 per person, not including the US$4 per person admission charge. Half-day tours take place either in morning (which photographers may prefer) or afternoon.

Otway is only about 70 kilometers northwest of Punta Arenas via Ruta 9 and a gravel road that leads west from a signed junction at the Carabineros Kon Aikén checkpoint; the gravel road passes the **Mina Pecket** coal mine before arriving at the *pingüinera*.

While the Otway colony is a worthwhile excursion, visitors with flexible schedules and a little more money should consider the larger Isla Magdalena colony in Monumento Natural Los Pingüinos, in the Strait of Magellan.

## ◖ MONUMENTO NATURAL LOS PINGÜINOS

From early October, more than 60,000 breeding pairs of Magellanic penguins paddle ashore and waddle to burrows that cover nearly all of 97-hectare Isla Magdalena, 20 nautical miles northeast of Punta Arenas, before returning to sea in April. Also the site of a landmark lighthouse, Isla Magdalena is the focal point of Monumento Natural Los Pingüinos, one of Conaf's smallest but most interesting reserves.

While the mainland Otway colony gets upwards of 40,000 visitors per year, Isla Magdalena gets fewer than 9,000—90 percent of

---

### PINGÜINOS AND PINGÜINERAS

Punta Arenas is close to two breeding colonies of the burrowing Magellanic penguin, *Spheniscus magellanicus*. The Otway Sound colony, about 45 minutes from the city, is interesting enough, but the larger colony on Isla Magdalena, in the Strait of Magellan, is two hours away by ferry or slightly less by bus and rigid inflatable.

Also known to English speakers as the jackass penguin because its call resembles that of a braying burro, the Magellanic is present from October to April. It's most numerous in January and February, when the chicks hatch in the sandy burrows that the birds have dug beneath the coastal turf. After the chicks have hatched, the parents alternate fishing trips for food that they later regurgitate to their young (combined with the scent of bird droppings, this makes any visit to a penguin colony an olfactory as well as a visual and auditory experience).

While the birds appear tame, they are wild animals and their sharp beaks can draw blood – maintain a respectful distance for photography. Though both colonies have fenced walking routes to restrain tourists, the birds themselves frequently cross these routes.

Besides the countless seabirds and dolphins en route, the Magdalena trip has the added bonus of a historic lighthouse that now serves as a visitors center on an island that's one big warren of penguin burrows. While neither trip is strenuous, any walk in Patagonia's roaring winds can be a workout.

them foreigners—because of its limited accessibility. In summer, though, the ferry *Melinka* visits the island three times weekly from Punta Arenas. Though more expensive than Otway tours, these excursions also offer the chance to see penguins and dolphins in the water, as well as black-browed albatrosses, cormorants, kelp gulls, skuas, South American terns, and other seabirds in the surrounding skies.

From a floating dock on the east side of the island, a short trail leads along the beach and up the hill to Scottish engineer George Slight's **Faro Magdalena** (1901), a lighthouse whose iron tower rises 13.5 meters above the island's highest point; still functioning, the light has a range of 10 nautical miles. A narrow spiral staircase ascends the tower.

In the building's first five decades, a resident caretaker maintained the acetylene light, but after its automation in 1955 the building was abandoned and vandalized. In 1981, though, the Chilean navy entrusted the building to Conaf; declared a national monument, it has since become a visitors center. It boasts remarkably good exhibits on the island's history (discovery, early navigation, cartography, and the lighthouse's construction) and natural history in both Spanish and English (though the English text is less complete). U.S. archaeologist Junius Bird, best known for his 1930s work at the mainland site of Pali Aike, also undertook excavations here.

For ferry excursions to Isla Magdalena, contact **Turismo Comapa** (Magallanes 990, tel. 061/200200, fax 061/225804, tcomapa@entelchile.net). In December, January, and February, after its regular Tuesday/Thursday/Saturday run to Porvenir, the *Melinka* makes a passengers-only trip to Isla Magdalena (US$33 pp, half that for children) from Terminal Tres Puentes; sailing time is 4 P.M. (bring food—the *Melinka*'s snack bar is pretty dire). Visitors spend about 1.5 hours on the island, returning to Punta Arenas around 9:30 P.M.

Passengers on the luxury *Mare Australis* and *Via Australis* cruises through Tierra del Fuego's fjords stop here on the return leg of the trip, but there's also an intermediate alternative that's more frequent than either of the above.

**Solo Expediciones** (José Nogueira 1255, tel. 061/243354, www.soloexpediciones.net) offers half-day excursions (US$58 pp) that shuttle passengers from the mainland in Zodiacs and include an approach to nearby Isla Marta, where the overflow from penguin-saturated Magdalena has migrated.

## FUERTE BULNES

In 1584, Spanish explorer Pedro Sarmiento de Gamboa organized an expedition of 15 ships and 4,000 men to control the Strait of Magellan, but after a series of disasters only three ships with 300 colonists arrived to found **Ciudad del Rey don Felipe**, at Punta Santa Ana south of present-day Punta Arenas. Even worse for the Spaniards, the inhospitable climate and unsuitable soils made agriculture impossible; when British privateer Thomas Cavendish landed three years later, in 1587, he found only a handful of survivors and gave it the name Port Famine, which survived as the Spanish **Puerto del Hambre.**

For many years, the consensus was that starvation alone determined the fate of Puerto Hambre, but Punta Arenas historian Mateo Martinic has suggested that disease, mutual acts of violence, Tehuelche attacks, and a simple sense of anguish or abandonment contributed to its demise. Unfortunately, the Chilean military control much of the area, making archaeological excavations that might resolve the question difficult.

The area remained unsettled until 1843, when President Manuel Bulnes ordered the cutter *Ancud* south from Chiloé with tools, construction materials, food, and livestock to take possession for the expansionist Chilean state. The result was Fuerte Bulnes, a military outpost that survived only a little longer than the original Spanish settlement before being relocated to Punta Arenas in 1848.

Modern Fuerte Bulnes, on the site of the first Chilean settlement, is a national monument more for its site than for its reconstructions of 19th-century buildings and the defensive walls—with sharpened stakes—that surround them. Among the structures were residences, stables, a blockhouse, a chapel, a jail, and warehouse.

Archaeologists located nearby remnants of Ciudad del Rey don Felipe in 1955, and later excavations turned up human remains, bullets, tombs, and ruins of Puerto Hambre's church. A relatively recent plaque (1965) celebrates the 125th anniversary of the Pacific Steam Navigation Company's ships *Chile* and *Perú* and their routes around the Horn.

Puerto Hambre and Fuerte Bulnes are 58 kilometers south of Punta Arenas via Ruta 9, which is paved about halfway; the rest is bumpy but always passable. There is no regular public transportation, but most Punta Arenas tour operators offer half-day excursions. Admission is free of charge.

## PARQUE MARINO FRANCISCO COLOANE

Established in July 2003, named for a Chilean author who chronicled the southern seas, this 67,000-hectare maritime park is the result of five years' biological investigations that pinpointed the area around Isla Carlos III, in the southwestern Strait of Magellan, as summer feeding grounds for the southern humpback whale. In addition to the humpbacks, which migrate the length of the South American coast from Colombia, the park's seas and shorelines are home to breeding populations of Magellanic penguins, cormorants, many other southern seabirds, fur seals, and sea lions. Orcas are also present.

From mid-December to late April, **Whalesound** (Pedro Montt 840, Punta Arenas, tel. 061/221076 or 099/3493862, www.whale sound.com) offers three-day expeditions (US$700 pp, minimum two persons) to the park, where guests sleep in geodesic dome tents, with comfortable Japanese beds and solar-powered electricity, on Isla Carlos III. The cost includes daily excursions with specialized bilingual guides and gourmet meals from a French-trained Chilean chef. Sea kayaks are also available.

## RÍO VERDE

Some 43 kilometers north of Punta Arenas on Ruta 9, a gravel road loops northwest along Seno Otway to Seno Skyring and Estancia Río Verde, which has seemingly made the transition from a shipshape sheep farm to a model municipality of exquisitely maintained public buildings in the Magellanic style. Note particularly the manicured gardens surrounding the **Escuela Básica,** the local boarding school.

Off to a good start, in one wing of the boarding school, the **Museo Comunal Río Verde** has exhibits on local history, natural history (taxidermy), ethnology, and local and regional literature. Hours are 10 A.M.–5 P.M. daily; admission costs US$1.

Unfortunately, the recently created Municipalidad burned to the ground a couple years back and destroyed some museum exhibits. Municipal offices have since moved to the former Hostería Río Verde, 90 kilometers from Punta Arenas and six kilometers south of the *estancia.*

Across from the former *hostería,* a small ferry shuttles vehicles and passengers to **Isla Riesco** (warning: it's free to the island, but costs US$30 to get your vehicle back to the mainland). Nearby, Paola Vizzani González's **Escultura Monumental,** a beached whale built of concrete and driftwood, honors the region's early colonists. Also nearby, the **Hito El Vapor** marks the final resting place of the steamer *Los Amigos,* which carried coal to outlying farms until it ran aground in a storm.

The loop road rejoins Ruta 9 at Villa Tehuelches, a wide spot in the road about 90 kilometers from Punta Arenas. This makes a good alternative route north or south for both motorists and mountain bikers.

While the *hostería* at the ferry crossing no longer provides accommodations, the Chilean-Uruguayan ◖ **Estancia Río Verde** (Km 98 Norte, tel. 061/311123 or 061/311131, jmma@ entelchile.net, US$70/90 s/d) offers stylish accommodations (one suite has a sunny tower with sea and pampas views), day tours that can include horseback riding and fishing, and *asados,* lunches, and tea in its restaurant. Open November to March, and a bargain by *estancia* standards, it also has gracious English-speaking ownership.

## ESTANCIA RÍO PENITENTE

Founded by Falkland Islands immigrants in 1891, Río Penitente has turned one of the best-preserved historic houses on any Patagonian sheep ranch into a guesthouse that feels like a step back in time, but still has essential comforts such as private baths. Most guest rooms in this two-story Victorian have period furniture, in immaculate condition, and fireplaces for heat. Activities include horseback riding and fly-fishing in its namesake river, but it's an ideal place for just relaxing. The restaurant serves lamb-on-a-stake barbecues to tour groups on weekends in particular.

Hostería Estancia Río Penitente (Ruta 9 Km 137, tel. 061/331694, www.hosteriariopenitente.com, US$100/120 s/d with breakfast) is open October to Semana Santa (Holy Week).

## ESTANCIA SAN GREGORIO

From a highway junction about 45 kilometers north of Punta Arenas, paved Ruta 225 leads east-northeast to the Argentine border at Monte Aymond, passing the former Estancia San Gregorio, once one of Chilean Patagonia's largest landholdings. Part of the Menéndez wool empire, San Gregorio dates from the 1890s, though it reached its peak between 1910 and 1930. Besides wool, it produced frozen mutton, hides, and tallow.

Now run as a cooperative, 120 kilometers from Punta Arenas, San Gregorio is a *zona típica* national historical monument. It exemplified the Anglo-Scottish model of the Patagonian sheep *estancia,* in which each unit was a self-sufficient hierarchy with a nearly omnipotent administrator at the top. Geographically, it consisted of discrete residential and production sectors: the former included the administrator's house, employee residences, shearers' dormitories, chapel, and the like, while the latter consisted of the shearing shed, warehouses, a smithery, company store, and similarly functional buildings. It had its own railroad and a pier to move the wool clip directly to freighters.

Most of San Gregorio's constructions date from the 1890s, but a descendent of the Menén-dez dynasty still occupies French architect Antoine Beaulier's **Casa Patronal** (1925). The farm featured an extensive system of windbreaks ranging upwards of five meters in height, later planted with Monterey cypress for beautification.

While technically not open to the public, many of San Gregorio's buildings line both sides of the highway to Monte Aymond. Beached on shore are the corroded hulks of the British clipper *Ambassador* (a national monument) and the company steamer *Amadeo,* which gave up the ghost in the 1940s.

## KIMIRI AIKE AND VICINITY

About 30 kilometers east of San Gregorio, paved Ruta 257 leads southeast to **Punta Delgada,** the port for the ferry crossing to Tierra del Fuego via the Primera Angostura narrows. Depending sometimes on tidal conditions, the ferries *Fueguino* and *Pionero* shuttle across the channel every 1.5 hours 8:30 A.M.–11 P.M. Fares are US$2.50 per person for passengers, US$1.25 for kids ages 10–14, US$22 for automobiles, and US$6.50 for motorcycles. Most buses to Argentine Tierra del Fuego use this route because the longer ferry to Porvenir goes only once daily, and is subject to delays or cancellation for rough seas.

At the highway junction, **Hostería Tehuelche** (tel. 061/1983006, sergioscabini@hotmail.com, US$50/59 s/d) was once the *casco* (big house) for the British-run Estancia Kimiri Aike; now, November–May, it offers satisfactory but overpriced accommodations in huge rooms with shared bath. Buses between Punta Arenas and Río Gallegos often stop here for lunch; breakfast, dinner, and snacks are also available. The Barros Luco sandwich can be good, but insist that they hold the mayonnaise.

## ◖ PARQUE NACIONAL PALI AIKE

Hugging the Argentine border north of Kimiri Aike and west of the Monte Aymond border crossing, little-visited Pali Aike is an area of volcanic steppe and rugged lava beds that once

guanacos, Parque Nacional Pali Aike, Chile

supported megafauna such as the ground sloth milodon and the native American horse, both of which disappeared soon after humans first inhabited the area some 11,000 years ago.

While Paleo-Indian hunters may have contributed to their extinction, environmental changes after the last major glaciation may also have played a role. In the 1930s, self-taught archaeologist Junius Bird, of New York's American Museum of Natural History, conducted the earliest systematic excavations of Paleo-Indian sites such as Cueva Pali Aike, within the park boundaries, and Cueva Fell, a short distance west. These archaeologically rich volcanic shelters (not caves in the strictest sense of the word) are the prime reason Chilean authorities have nominated the area as a UNESCO World Heritage Site.

Findings at Pali Aike include human remains that have yielded insights on Paleo-Indian funerary customs, while materials from Cueva Fell have helped reveal the transition from relatively simple hunting to more complex forms of subsistence. These include sophisticated hunting tools such as the bow and arrow and *boleadoras,* and a greater reliance on

coastal and marine resources. There are also indicators of ceremonial artifacts.

## Geography and Climate

Part of arid eastern Magallanes, 5,030-hectare Pali Aike consists of rolling steppe grasslands whose porous volcanic soils and slag absorb water quickly. Almost constant high winds and cool temperatures make it a better summer or autumn excursion.

## Flora and Fauna

While the milodon and native horse may have disappeared, the park's grasslands swarm with herds of wild guanaco and flocks of rheas, upland geese, *bandurria* (ibis), and other birds. Pumas and foxes are the major predators.

## Sights and Recreation

Accessible by road, **Cueva Pali Aike** is a volcanic tube seven meters wide and five meters high at its mouth; it is 17 meters deep but tapers as it advances. In the 1930s, Bird discovered both human and megafauna remains, at least 8,600 years old and probably much older, in the cave.

Tours from Punta Arenas visit Cueva Pali Aike and usually hike the 1.7-kilometer trail through the **Escorial del Diablo** (the appropriately named Devil's Slag Heap, which is hell on hiking boots). The trail ends at the volcanic **Crater Morada del Diablo.**

From Cueva Pali Aike, a nine-kilometer footpath leads to **Laguna Ana,** where waterfowl are abundant, and the main road, five kilometers from the park entrance. Mountain bikes should be ideal for this sort of rolling terrain, but it could be even tougher on tires than it is on boots.

## Practicalities

A campground is presumably in the works, but there are no tourist services as yet, so bring supplies.

At the main entrance, Conaf has a ranger station but collects no admission fee. A great destination for solitude seekers, Pali Aike officially gets fewer than 1,200 visitors per annum, only a quarter of them foreigners.

Parque Nacional Pali Aike is 196 kilometers northeast of Punta Arenas via Ruta 9, Ruta 255, and a graveled secondary road from the hamlet of Cooperativa Villa O'Higgins, 11 kilometers beyond Kimiri Aike. Just south of the Chilean border post at Monte Aymond, a hard-to-follow dirt road also leads to the park.

There is no public transportation, but Punta Arenas travel agencies can arrange visits. Hiring a car, though, is probably the best option, especially if shared among several people.

## ◖ THE FJORDS OF FUEGIA

Short of Antarctica itself, some of the Southern Hemisphere's most awesome scenery occurs in the Beagle Channel and southern Tierra del Fuego. And as usual, Charles Darwin left one of the most vivid descriptions of the channel named for the vessel on which he sailed:

> The scenery here becomes even grander than before. The lofty mountains on the north side compose the granitic axis, or backbone of the country, and boldly rise to a height of between three and four thousand feet, with one peak above six thousand feet. They are covered by a wide mantle of perpetual snow, and numerous cascades pour their waters, through the woods, into the narrow channel below. In many parts, magnificent glaciers extend from the mountain side to the water's edge. It is scarcely possible to imagine anything more beautiful than the beryl-like blue of these glaciers, and especially as contrasted with the dead white of the upper expanse of the snow. The fragments which had fallen from the glacier into the water, were floating away, and the channel with the icebergs presented, for the space of a mile, a miniature likeness of the Polar Sea.

Even today, fairly few visitors see Tierra del Fuego's splendid fjords, barely changed since Darwin described them in 1833; many of those do so on board week-long excursions from Punta Arenas to the Argentine port of Ushuaia and back on the twin Chilean vessels *Mare Australis* and *Via Australis.* Unlike the Navimag ferry from Puerto Montt to Puerto Natales, these are cruises in the traditional sense—the passengers are waited on hand and foot, and they're not cheap. Yet for the foreseeable future, this remains the only way to see the area short of sailing your own yacht or chartering someone else's, and for that reason it's worth consideration even for those with limited finances.

One common alternative is to do either leg of the voyage separately—either four days, three nights from Punta Arenas to Ushuaia, or five days, four nights from Ushuaia to Punta Arenas. The boats sometimes undertake variants that involve four nights from Punta Arenas and three from Ushuaia, and there's usually some duplication; both legs, for instance, visit the western Beagle Channel's **Glaciar Pía,** and sometimes the boats are there simultaneously.

Routes can vary depending on weather conditions in this notoriously capricious climate. After an evening departure from Punta Arenas's Muelle Prat, the vessel crosses the Strait of Magellan to enter the **Seno del**

**Almirantazgo** (Admiralty Sound), a westward maritime extension of the freshwater Lago Fagnano trough. Passengers usually go ashore at **Bahía Ainsworth**, near the **Glaciar Marinelli**, where there's a short hiking trail through what was once forest until feral beavers dammed the area into a series of ponds; the most interesting site for most visitors is a small elephant seal colony. Farther west, at **Isla Tucker**, there's a small Magellanic penguin colony (usually observed from an inflatable Zodiac) and it's also possible to see the rare striated caracara, *Phalcoboenus australis.*

After a night's sailing, the ship may enter the **Fiordo D'Agostini**, a glacial inlet named for the Italian priest and mountaineer who explored the Cordillera Darwin's farthest recesses in the early 20th century. When high winds make it impossible to approach the **Glaciar Serrano** (named for Chilean naval Lieutenant Ramón Serrano Montaner, who charted the strait in 1879), an option is the more sheltered **Glaciar D'Agostini**. Even here, though, seracs crack off the glacier's face, touching off a rapid surge of water and ice that runs parallel to a broad gravel beach and, when it subsides, leaves the beach littered with boulders of ice.

Darwin, again, described the dangers of travel in a land that sea kayakers are just beginning to explore:

> The boats being hauled on shore at our dinner hour, we were admiring from the distance of half a mile a perpendicular cliff of ice, and were wishing that some more fragments would fall. At last, down came a mass with a roaring noise, and immediately we saw the smooth outline of a wave traveling toward us. The men ran down as quickly as they could to the boats; for the chance of their being dashed to pieces was evident. One of the seamen just caught hold of the bows, as the curling breaker reached it: he was knocked over and over, but not hurt; and the boats, though thrice lifted on high and let fall again, received no damage.... I had previously noted that some large fragments of rock on the beach had been lately displaced; but until seeing this wave, I did not understand the cause.

After navigating Canal Cockburn, where open ocean swells can rock the boat at least briefly, the vessel turns into the calmer **Canal Ocasión** and eventually enters the Beagle Channel's north arm, sailing past the so-called **Avenida de los Glaciares**, a series of glaciers named for various European countries; passengers normally disembark at **Glaciar Pía**. Traditionally, after sailing through the night, the ship has spent a few hours at **Puerto Williams** as Chilean authorities came aboard to process passports before it continued to Argentina, but emigration formalities now take place at **Puerto Navarino**, at the western end of **Isla Navarino**.

Proceeding to **Ushuaia**, all passengers spend the night aboard; those returning to Punta Arenas have the day free in Ushuaia before returning to the ship, while new passengers check their bags downtown before boarding in late afternoon.

After reentering Chile at Puerto Navarino, the ship sails south to **Cabo de Hornos** (Cape Horn) and, wind permitting (less than 45 knots), passengers disembark to visit the small Chilean naval detachment and hike to the stylized albatross sculpture that symbolizes sailors who lost their lives "rounding the Horn."

Again, if weather permits, the captain can choose to round the Horn himself before proceeding north to **Bahía Wulaia**, on Isla Navarino's western shore. Here passengers visit the site of an early mission where, in a notorious incident, the Yámana massacred all but one of the Anglicans and their crew. There is then the option of a short but steep hike with panoramic views of the bay, or an easier shoreline walk with birdlife including Magellanic oystercatchers.

Returning to the Beagle Channel, the ships turns westward through the Beagle Channel's north arm, again passing the Avenida de los Glaciares and entering Fiordo Pía (Pía Fjord), where dozens of waterfalls cascade down sheer metamorphic slopes from the **Glaciar Pía** and passengers take a short hike. Proceeding through the afternoon and the night, the boat starts the last full day navigating the **Fiordo Chico** (Little Fjord), where passengers board Zodiacs to approach but not land at **Glaciar Plüschow**, named for a German pioneer aviator who took the first aerial photos of the Cordillera Darwin.

In the afternoon, the **Glaciar Águila** is the site of an easy shoreline walk or a more demanding slog through knee-deep mud in a southern beech forest (the video footage of this hike, shown the night before in an orientation session, is priceless). On the final morning, the boat sails north to **Isla Magdalena** before returning to Punta Arenas.

## Practicalities

Well-organized without being regimented, the cruise is informal in terms of dress and behavior. At the start, passengers sign up for meal tables; places are fixed for the duration except at the buffet breakfast, when people tend to straggle in at different times. In general, passengers are grouped according to language, though they often place together people who speak English as a second language. The staff themselves can handle Spanish, English, German, French, and occasionally other languages.

After introduction of the captain and crew, and an obligatory safety drill, there's a welcome drink and a brief folklore show (in Punta Arenas) or tango demonstration (in Ushuaia). Smoking is prohibited everywhere except outdoors and at the rear of the fourth deck pub; bar consumption is now included in the package.

The cabins themselves are reasonably spacious, with either a double or twin beds, built-in reading lights, a closet with hangers and a small lock box for valuables, and a private bath with excellent hot showers. Some rooms also have a fold-down bunk for children or a third person. The food is abundant and occasionally excellent, though breakfasts are a little monotonous;

the wine is superb, and the service exceptional. Vegetarian menus are available on request.

For those who tire of the landscape or when the weather is bad, onboard activities include karaoke, PowerPoint lectures on flora and fauna, engine-room tours, and culinary demonstrations of carved cucumbers, peppers, zucchinis, and other vegetables, in the shapes of birds and flowers. The farewell dinner is a fairly gala affair, followed by champagne on the topmost deck.

Punta Arenas is the home port for fjord-bound cruises; check-in takes place at Turismo Comapa (Magallanes 990, tel. 061/200200) 1–5 P.M., while boarding takes place 5–6 P.M. at the entrance to Muelle Prat. Some passengers begin or end the trip in Argentine Tierra del Fuego, where check-in takes place at Comapa's Ushuaia office (San Martín 245, tel. 02901/430727) 9 A.M.–4 P.M.; boarding takes place at the Muelle Commercial 5–6 P.M.

Usually this very popular cruise runs full October–April, except for the last trip before Christmas, which may be only half full; in this case, it may be possible to negotiate a deal in Punta Arenas, getting a private cabin without paying a single supplement, for instance. In addition, at this time of year, days are so long that it's possible to enjoy the landscape until after 11 P.M., and there's sufficient light to read by 4 A.M.

Make reservations through **Cruceros Australis** (Avenida Bosque Norte 0440, 11th floor, Las Condes, Santiago, tel. 02/4423110, fax 02/2035173, www.australis.com), which also has offices in Buenos Aires (Carlos Pellegrini 989, 6th floor, Retiro, tel. 011/4325-8400) and in Miami (4014 Chase Ave., Suite 202, Miami Beach, FL 33140, tel. 305/695-9618 or 877/678-3772). Per-person rates for four days and three nights start at US$960–1,680 in low season up to US$1,140–1,980 in high season. For five days and four nights, the comparable rates are US$1,110–1,940 in low season to US$1,310–2,290 in high season.

# Puerto Natalesle

In the past 20 years, Puerto Natales has changed from a sleepy wool and fishing port on what seemed the aptly named Seno Última Esperanza—"Last Hope Sound"—to a bustling tourist town whose season has lengthened well beyond the traditional summer months of January and February. Its proximity to the famous Parque Nacional Torres del Paine, coupled with its status as the southern terminus for the scenic ferry route from Puerto Montt, has placed it on the international travel map, utterly transforming the local economy.

While Natales has no knockout attractions in its own right, the town enjoys a magnificent seaside setting, with the snow-capped Cordillera Sarmiento and Campo de Hielo Sur, the southern Patagonian ice cap, visible over the water to the west, and the waterfront is far more presentable than in the past. For visitors to Paine and other regional sights, it has abundant services, including tour operators and rental equipment, while there are also convenient connections to the Argentine

town of El Calafate and Parque Nacional Los Glaciares.

In the aftermath of Argentina's economic meltdown of 2001–2002, though, Natales took a triple hit: retired Chilean coal miners from Río Turbio saw their incomes trapped in frozen Argentine accounts and their pensions cut by two-thirds because of the Argentine devaluation and Chile's own strong peso, even as their own cost of living remained high, and active workers have seen their wages decline. At the same time, local merchants have seen their Argentine business dry up as merchandise is no longer cheaper on the Chilean side. Only tourism remains reliable, but the strong peso has made Chile more expensive and visitors are spending shorter periods here. Some worry that a recent hotel construction boom may create overcapacity and drive down prices.

One possible strong point is the possible construction of a 150-meter cruise-ship pier, which would simplify land transfers from both

# PUERTO NATALES

**Estero Natales**

To Cerro Dorotea, Puerto Bories, Cueva del Milodón,
Punta Arenas, and Parque Nacional Torres del Paine

**Seno Última Esperanza**

MUELLE
(FERRY DOCK)

SEE "PLAZA DE ARMAS
ARTURO PRAT" MAP

Plaza de
Armas
Arturo Prat

Plaza
Primero
de Mayo

SERNATUR

HOSTAL DRAKE

CASA CECILIA

HOSTAL ISLA MORENO

HOTEL MARTIN GUSINDE

HOSTAL DOS LAGUNAS

LAVANDERÍA
CANCH

HOSTAL AMERINDIA

CHILE
NATIVO

CAMBIOS SUR

CENTRO ESPAÑOL

HOTEL
AQUATERRA

BIG FOOT
ADVENTURE PATAGONIA

ANTARES
PATAGONIA

RESIDENCIAL
SUTHERLAND

HOSTAL NATALES

PATAGONIA DULCE

CALETA
GASTRONÓMICA

LOS
VIAJEROS

MUSEO
HISTÓRICO
MUNICIPAL

HOTEL INDIGO PATAGONIA
CAFÉ ÍNDIGO

LOS PIONEROS

HOTEL GLACIARES

HOTEL
CHARLES
DARWIN

HOSTAL DE LOS
CASTILLOS

EL MARÍTIMO

HOTEL COSTA
AUSTRALIS

EXPRESS RENT A CAR

HOTEL SALTOS DEL PAINE

CAFÉ
ANDRÉS

HOTEL LADY
FLORENCE DIXIE

SERVITUR

RESIDENCIAL
JOSMAR

CONAF

HOSPEDAJE
TERESA RUIZ

HOSPITAL
PUERTO NATALES

ENTEL

HOTEL
LAGUNA
AZUL

TURISMO
VIENTO SUR

BUSES
COOTRA

THE DRIED
FRUIT GUY

HOSTAL DON
GUILLERMO

BUSES
FERNÁNDEZ

RESIDENCIAL
MARÍA JOSÉ

CEMENTERIO

HOSTAL NANCY

BUSES PACHECO

BUS SUR

BAQUEANO
ZAMORA/BUSES SUR

ERRATIC
ROCK

**Streets:** VALDIVIA, MANUEL BULNES, ANGAMOS, PHILLIPI, BLANCO ENCALADA, ESMERALDA, CHORRILLOS, E. RAMÍREZ, GALVARINO, SÁNCHEZ, SEÑORET, ARANA, BARROS, BORIES, MAGALLANES, TOMÁS ROGERS, EBERHARD, MANUEL BULNES, ARTURO PRAT, O'HIGGINS, MIRAFLORES, YUNGAY, CARRERA PINTO, SARGENTO ALDEA, RIQUELME, BAQUEDANO, PASAJE MILITAR, LADRILLEROS, HURTADO DE MENDOZA, PEDRO MONTT

0   200 yds
0   200 m

© AVALON TRAVEL PUBLISHING, INC.

the ferry (which does have an improved dock) and visiting cruisers, but it's still at the talking stage. Meanwhile, private initiative has built a smaller jetty for local cruises near Puerto Bories, north of town.

On the eastern shores of Seno Último Esperanza, Puerto Natales (pop. 16,978) is 250 kilometers northwest of Punta Arenas via paved Ruta 9. It is 150 kilometers south of Parque Nacional Torres del Paine, also by Ruta 9, which is paved for 13 kilometers north of the city.

## HISTORY

Última Esperanza acquired its name because expeditions led by the 16th-century Spaniards Juan Ladrilleros and Pedro Sarmiento de Gamboa failed to find a westbound route to the Pacific here. Puerto Natales proper dates from the early 20th century, a few years after German explorer Hermann Eberhard founded the area's first sheep *estancia* at Puerto Prat. Within a few years, the Sociedad Explotadora de Tierra del Fuego had built a slaughterhouse at nearby Bories to process and pack mutton for the export market. While the livestock economy declined in the second half of the 20th century, the tourist boom has reactivated and diversified the economy.

## SIGHTS

The Sociedad Explotadora de Tierra del Fuego, which owned large tracts of pasture in both Chile and Argentina, financed construction of Natales' gingerbread-style **Municipalidad,** dating from 1929 (many might have said the powerful Sociedad Explotadora was the region's de facto government). Immediately east, the **Iglesia Parroquial María Auxiliadora** dates from the same era and shares its Magellanic style.

In the same exterior fashion but with a roomier interior that displays its holdings to advantage, the **Museo Histórico Municipal** (Bulnes 285, tel. 061/411263, muninata@ ctcinternet.cl) offers displays on natural history, archaeology, and the region's aboriginal peoples, European settlement, and the rural economy (including the Sociedad Explotadora), Puerto Natales's own urban evolution, and the

Carabineros police, who played a role in the museum's creation. Noteworthy individual artifacts include a Yámana (Yahgan) dugout canoe and Aónikenk (Tehuelche) *boleadoras,* plus historical photographs of Captain Eberhard and the town's development. Hours are 8:30 A.M.–12:30 P.M. and 2:30–6 P.M. weekdays, 3–6 P.M. weekends. Admission costs US$1 for Chileans, US$2 for foreigners.

## ENTERTAINMENT

Puerto Natales's nightlife is limited mostly to dining out and to low-key bars such as **Café Indigo** (Ladrilleros 105), a Chilean-run but gringo-oriented gathering place with nightly slide shows about Natales and Torres del Paine.

**El Bar de Ruperto** (Bulnes 371) takes its name from the pisco-swilling burro once popular on Chilean TV ads.

## SHOPPING

There are two locations for **Ñandú Artesanía** (Bulnes 599, tel. 061/415660; Eberhard 586, tel. 061/414382, www.nanduartesania.cl), which sells maps and books in addition to a selection of quality crafts. **World's End** (Blanco Encalada 226, tel. 061/414725) is a map specialist.

The **Pueblo Artesanal Ehterh Aike** (Philippi 660) has a variety of crafts but is also the best place in town to buy fresh fruit and other produce.

## ACCOMMODATIONS

Over the past two decades-plus, Puerto Natales has developed one of Chile's densest offerings of accommodations. This is especially true in the budget category, where competition keeps prices low, and in exceptional new upscale options—but there are plenty of mediocre and ordinary places in all ranges. Off-season rates can drop dramatically at upscale places.

### US$10-25

In new quarters, **Residencial María José** (Esmeralda 869, tel. 061/412218, juan_lasa@hot mail.com, US$8 pp) is Natales's Israeli favorite. **Residencial Josmar** (Esmeralda 517, tel. 061/414417, US$8.50 pp) has also built a spacious campground (US$4 pp) with clearly delineated sites, privacy from the street, electricity, and hot showers. **Magallania Backpacker** (Tomás Rogers 255, tel. 061/414950, magallania@yahoo.com, US$9 pp) is an informal hostel-style facility with spacious dorms and a few doubles (US$25) including breakfast, kitchen privileges, a TV room, and *buena onda* (good vibes).

**Hospedaje Teresa Ruiz** (Esmeralda 463, tel. 061/410472, freepatagonia@hotmail.com, US$9 pp) gets high marks for congeniality, cleanliness, and outstanding breakfasts with homemade rhubarb preserves.

Relocated in improved quarters, **Hostal Nancy** (Ramírez 540, tel. 061/410022, www.nataleslodge.cl, US$9 pp with breakfast) has long been a popular choice in its price range.

The local HI affiliate is **Albergue Path@gone** (Eberhard 595, tel. 061/413291, pathgone@entelchile.net, US$11 pp), which has very good facilities. **Residencial Sutherland** (Barros Arana 155, tel. 061/410359, US$8 pp, US$22 d) has recently added rooms with private bath.

Run by expatriate Oregonians, the informal hostel **Erratic Rock** (Baquedano 719, tel. 061/410355, www.erraticrock.com, US$11 pp) occupies a creaky house with character. It also serves a better-than-average breakfast, has a large book exchange, and rents quality gear for Paine-bound travelers.

Friendly **Residencial Patagonia Aventura** (Tomás Rogers 179, tel. 061/411028, info@apatagonia.com, US$12 pp) provides a bit more privacy than others in its range, with knowledgeable operators who also rent equipment.

## US$25-50

In an older house with substantial character, steadily improving ◖ **Hostal Dos Lagunas** (Barros Arana 104, tel. 061/415733, doslagunas@hotmail.com, US$17 pp with shared bath) is fast becoming a favorite; rates include an ample and varied breakfast.

Stuck in an off-the-beaten-sidewalk location, looking more expensive than it is, the immaculate ◖ **Hostal Don Guillermo** (O'Higgins 657, tel./fax 061/414506, US$15/26 s/d–US$45 d) is seriously underpriced compared to nearby competitors. Though the singles are small, some rooms now have private baths and the breakfast is excellent; rates vary according to whether the room has cable TV.

At friendly **Hostal Dickson** (Bulnes 307, tel. 061/411871, patagoniadickson@hotmail.com, US$22–28 d with shared bath, US$37 d with private bath), look at the rooms closely—some have windows so small that they're more like jail cells. On the other hand, there's central heating, the beds are good, the shared baths are numerous, and rates include breakfast.

Opened in late 2005, **Hostel Natales** (Ladrilleros 209, tel. 061/410081, www.hostelnatales.cl, US$20 pp, US$37/46 s/d) transformed the aging Hotel Palace into warm, luminous accommodations with private bath; some rooms have two or four bunk beds, while others have standard doubles for couples. The lobby and atrium (which includes a fountain) are spacious and inviting, with comfortable chairs and sofas, but the rooms are sparsely furnished and sounds carry from the lobby (which is also an Internet café with balky WiFi) to the nearest ones. An ample breakfast costs US$5 extra.

## US$50-100

Now a Natales institution, ◖ **Casa Cecilia** (Tomás Rogers 60, tel. 061/411797, www.casaceciliahostal.com, US$19/33–43/52 s/d) deserves credit for improving accommodations standards here—it's such a legend that, on occasion, nonguests even ask for tours of the hospitable Swiss-Chilean bed-and-breakfast. The rooms are simple, and some are small, but all enjoy central heating, some have private bath and cable TV, and the cheerful atrium is a popular gathering place. Rates include the usual sumptuous breakfast.

Rehabbed **Hostal Drake** (Philippi 383, tel./fax 061/411553, www.hostalfrancisdrake.com, US$45/57 s/d) is a comfortable hostelry in a quiet location that tour operators often choose for their clients. Rates include breakfast, but you may need persistence to get IVA discounts.

Opened in early 2006, **Hostal Amerindia** (Barros Arana 135, tel. 061/411945, www.amerindiapatagonia.com, US$40–60 s or d, with a 6 percent surcharge for credit cards) is an artfully decorated five-room bed-and-breakfast. Its major shortcoming is that three otherwise comfortable rooms share one bath, though the other two have private baths. It also has WiFi and serves a buffet breakfast.

With what may be Natales's most colorful garden—the summer roses are a sight—**Hostal de los Castillos** (Bulnes 241, tel. 061/413641, www.hostalcastillos.com, US$46/65 s/d with breakfast) is also a popular teahouse. The rooms themselves are comfortable and spacious, though one picture-window double faces the street (heavy curtains give it sufficient privacy).

**Hostal Isla Moreno** (Tomás Rogers 68, tel. 061/414773, US$46/65 s/d) enjoys fine natural light in modern rooms with private bath; a couple lack exterior windows but have skylights). It also has a restaurant with a limited nightly menu.

The striking **( Hotel Lady Florence Dixie** (Manuel Bulnes 659, tel. 061/411158, florence@chileanpatagonia.com, US$61/76–72/87 s/d) has expanded and upgraded what was already a good hotel without becoming a budget-breaker. **Hotel Glaciares** (Eberhard 104, tel./fax 061/411452, www.hotelglaciares.com, US$89/99 s/d) is also a respectable option.

Atop a bluff on the Paine road just north of town, **Weskar Patagonian Lodge** (Ruta 9 Km 1, tel. 061/414168, www.weskar.cl, US$89/99 s/d) has panoramic views of the sound from its bar/restaurant and slightly less panoramic views from its upstairs rooms, some of whose windows are triangular. The rooms themselves are midsize but get fine natural light, and the beds and other furnishings are excellent.

## US$100-200
Just a couple years ago **( Hotel Aquaterra** (Bulnes 299, tel. 061/412239, www.aquaterra patagonia.com, US$90/102 s/d), a purpose-built hotel that combines style (native woods) and substance (comfortable furnishings), was almost unique. Though the competition is

catching up, it's still worth consideration, as is its unconventional restaurant menu.

If only for honoring history's greatest scientist, **Hotel Charles Darwin** (Bulnes 90, tel. 061/412478, www.hotelcharlesdarwin.com, US$109/132 s/d) deserves some attention; painted in pastels, the 22 rooms range from smallish to midsize, but they're flooded with natural light and have state-of-the-art baths. Management is accommodating, and the restaurant has an interesting menu as well.

The handsome **Hotel Saltos del Paine** (Bulnes 156, tel. 061/413607, fax 061/410261, www.saltosdelpaine.cl, US$105/140 s/d) is more spacious than the Darwin. One of the best values in its category is the modern **( Hotel Martín Gusinde** (Bories 278, tel. 061/412770, www.martingusinde.cl, US$111/135 s/d). It is well located and has good service.

Natales's most distinctive new accommodations are at the subtly landscaped **Hotel Altiplánico del Sur** (Ruta 9 Norte, Huerto 258, tel. 061/412525, www.altiplanico.cl, US$160/170 s/d), which has built all its rooms into the hillside along the Paine highway about two kilometers north of town. Only the windows and roof rise above ground level, while blocks of peat insulate the concrete structure and help integrate it into its site. The common areas, the rooms, and the furnishings all display an elegant design simplicity.

Opened in late 2006, on the site of what was once a modest bed-and-breakfast, **Hotel Indigo Patagonia** (Ladrilleros 105, tel. 061/413609, www.indigopatagonia.com, US$135–190 s or d) is an audacious new hotel and spa with 29 rooms, including half a dozen suites. Facing the waterfront, it bids to help transform the shoreline.

## Over US$200
Rates at the waterfront classic **Hotel Costa Australis** (Costanera Pedro Montt 262, tel. 061/412000, www.costaustralis.cl, US$180/205–225/250 s/d) depend on whether the room has a city or sea view. It's hard-pressed, though, to keep up with newer choices such as the Altiplánico and Indigo.

## FOOD

Known for seafood, Natales has several moderately priced eateries and improving midrange to upscale choices.

To stock up on groceries, visit **Super Mix** (Bulnes 646, tel. 061/415358). More specialized, for your Paine trail mix, is **The Dried Fruit Guy** (Baquedano 443).

For freshly brewed coffee, tea, juices, sandwiches, and sweets, **Café Cielo de Palo** (Tomás Rogers 179, tel. 061/415636) keeps longer hours than most Natales eateries (7 A.M.–11 P.M.). Decor-free **Masay** (Bulnes 427, tel. 061/415008) has decent inexpensive sandwiches and pizzas.

**Café Evasión** (Eberhard 595-B, tel. 061/414605) is a moderately priced café-restaurant with daily lunch specials. Basic Chilean dishes outshine the Italian at **La Repizza** (Blanco Encalada 294, tel. 061/410361).

**Patagonia Dulce** (Barros Arana 233, tel. 061/415285, www.patagoniadulce.cl) serves several varieties of hot chocolate (expensive at around US$4–5 each, but welcome on a cold Natales morning) and desserts, including kuchen and mousses, along with rich homemade chocolate candies by weight. Unfortunately it doesn't open until 11 A.M.

On the east side of the Plaza de Armas, the British-run vegetarian 【 **El Living** (Arturo Prat 156, tel. 061/411140, US$4 for sandwiches) also serves breakfast, sandwiches (around US$4–5), and desserts (try especially the Sacher torte). Its owner arrived here by way of Torres del Paine's extravagant Hotel Salto Chico, but his food is more upmarket than his prices; hours are 11 A.M.–11 P.M. daily, but it closes May–mid-October.

Relying on their waterfront locations to draw crowds, **El Marítimo** (Pedro Montt 214, tel. 061/414994) and **Los Pioneros** (Pedro Montt 166, tel. 061/410783) offer good value for money. For better atmosphere, try the casual **La Tranquera** (Bulnes 579, tel. 061/411039).

**La Caleta Gastronómica** (Eberhard 261, tel. 061/413969) is a moderately priced (US$5–8) locale that offers excellent value—

try the salmon with king crab sauce. Another well-established option is **Café Andrés** (Ladrilleros 381, tel. 061/412380), for cooked-to-order seafood.

**Don Jorge** (Bories 430, tel. 061/410999) and **El Asador Patagónico** (Prat 158, tel. 061/413553) are both new *parrillas* facing the Plaza de Armas.

**La Burbuja** (Bulnes 300, tel. 061/414204) specializes in seafood and meats, but also has vegetarian offerings; try the *ostiones al pil pil* (US$6), a slightly spicy scallops appetizer, and the *congrio* (conger eel) for an entrée.

Offering exceptional views of the sound and a steadily improving menu, 【 **Café Indigo** (Ladrilleros 105, tel. 061/413609) prepares sandwiches, pastas, seafood dishes such as *chupe de centolla* (king crab soufflé), and a variety of vegetarian options.

In a relaxed setting, 【 **La Casa de Pepe** (Tomás Rogers 131, tel. 061/410950, www.lacasadepepe-chilespezialitaten.de) prepares refined versions of Chilean standards such as *pastel de choclo* (US$8.50) and *cazuela de ave* (US$7.50) with the freshest ingredients. On the Plaza de Armas, it's also 100-percent tobacco-free (though the owner himself is an occasional smoker).

Rarely does Chilean pizza merit special mention, but the thin-crusted pies at 【 **Mesita Grande** (Eberhard 508, tel. 061/411571, www.mesitagrande.cl) clearly do. Individual pizzas (US$5–9), of four ample slices, range from simple mozzarella to spinach and garlic to ground lamb and just about everything in between; diners sit at either of two long but solid tables that encourage conversation with their neighbors.

Greatly improved, opposite the plaza, 【 **La Oveja Negra** (Tomás Rogers 169, tel. 061/415711, US$6–10) is the choice for a quiet meal in relaxed, if not quite intimate, surroundings. For either seafood or beef, its upscale aspirations make for more elaborate dining than at most of its competitors.

Part of its eponymous hotel, **Aquaterra** (Bulnes 299, tel. 061/412239, US$9–12 for entrées) is an upscale restaurant with menu items such as Mexican fajitas and Japanese *gyoza* (pot stickers) rarely seen in this part of the world. For more conservative palates, it offers traditional beef dishes.

Underrated 〖 **Última Esperanza** (Eberhard 354, tel. 061/413626) deserves more attention than it gets for exceptional seafood at reasonable prices with outstanding service. **Los Viajeros** (Bulnes 291, tel. 061/411156) is a recent entry in the seafood category but also serves grilled Patagonian lamb. The **Centro Español** (Magallanes 247, tel. 061/411181) promises Spanish cuisine, but it remains a work in progress.

New in 2006, **Angélica's** (Eberhard 532, tel. 061/410365) is working to be a sophisticated option of the sort that Natales has always lacked, with items such as lamb with rosemary, green-pepper steak, corvina with a shrimp sauce, and king crab cannelloni. With most entrées upwards or well upwards of US$10, the price-quality ratio isn't there yet, but it's too early to write it off. The decor is pleasing but unremarkable, the aluminum-siding exterior uninviting, but the service is professional. The desserts, particularly the chocolate mousse (US$5.50), are first rate.

At Natales's best ice creamery, **Helados Bruna** (Bulnes 585), *calafate* and rhubarb are the regional specialties.

## INFORMATION

In a freestanding waterfront chalet, the Natales delegation of **Sernatur** (Pedro Montt 19, tel./fax 061/412125) is open 8:15 A.M.–7 P.M. weekdays all year; December–March, it's also open 10:30 A.M.–1:30 P.M. and 3–6 P.M. weekends. It has helpful personnel, occasionally English-speaking, and fairly thorough information on accommodations, restaurants, and transportation.

For national-park information, contact **Conaf** (O'Higgins 584, tel. 061/411438).

Two relocated Oregonians now publish the monthly freebie *Black Sheep,* with engagingly written articles and information on Natales, Torres del Paine, and services throughout the region. It's widely available around town.

## SERVICES

Puerto Natales has several exchange houses: **Cambio Mily** (Blanco Encalada 266), **Cambios Sur** (Eberhard 285), and **Stop Cambios** (Baquedano 380), at Hotel Laguna Azul. **Banco Santander Santiago** (Bulnes 598) has an ATM.

**Correos de Chile** (Eberhard 429), at the southwest corner of Plaza Arturo Prat, is the post office.

Long-distance operators include **Telefónica CTC** (Blanco Encalada and Bulnes) and **Entel** (Baquedano 270).

Internet connections are improving and cheapening. Try **World's End** (Blanco Encalada 226) for high-speed connections, but new outlets are appearing all the time.

**Servilaundry** (Bulnes 513, tel. 061/412869) or **Lavandería Catch** (Bories 218) can do the washing.

**Hospital Puerto Natales** (tel. 061/411582) is at Ignacio Carrera Pinto 537.

## GETTING THERE
### Air

LAN/LanExpress no longer has a separate office here, but **Turismo Comapa** (Bulnes 533, tel. 061/414300, fax 061/414361) handles reservations and tickets. Punta Arenas–bound buses will drop passengers at that city's Aeropuerto Presidente Carlos Ibáñez del Campo.

### Bus

There is frequent bus service to and from Punta Arenas and Torres del Paine, and regular but less frequent service to the Argentine destinations of Río Turbio, Río Gallegos, and El Calafate.

Carriers serving Punta Arenas (US$5.50, three hours) include **Bus Sur** (Baquedano 500, tel. 061/411859), **Buses Sur** (Baquedano 534, tel. 061/411325), **Buses Fernández** (Ramírez 399, tel. 061/411111), **Buses Pacheco** (Baquedano and O'Higgins, tel. 061/414513), and **Buses Transfer** (Bulnes 518, tel. 061/412616). Round-trip tickets offer small discounts, but less flexibility. Bus Sur goes to Ushuaia (Argentina) Tuesday and Friday at 7 A.M.

Services to Torres del Paine (US$12, two hours) vary seasonally, and there is frequent turnover among the agencies; again, there are small discounts for round-trip fares. Carriers include **Buses JB** (Prat 258, tel. 061/412824), **Buses Fortaleza** (Prat 234, tel. 061/410595), **Buses María José** (Bulnes 386, tel. 061/414312), and **Bus Sur. Turismo Viento Sur** (Baquedano 414, tel. 061/613840, puertonatales@vientosur.com) operates a daily door-to-door service (US$28 pp) as far as Hostería Lago Grey.

For the Argentine border town of Río Turbio (US$2, one hour), where there are connections to El Calafate and Río Gallegos, try **Buses Cootra** (Baquedano 454, tel. 061/412785), which has five to seven daily except on weekends, when there are only two or three. Bus Sur has fewer departures.

To the Argentine town of El Calafate (US$17, 5.5 hours), the carriers are Buses Cootra, Bus Sur, and **Turismo Zaahj** (Prat 236, tel. 061/412260). While these services are frequent in high season, in winter they may be weekly only.

### Ferry

**Turismo Comapa/Navimag** (Bulnes 533, tel. 061/414300, www.navimag.com) operates the weekly car/passenger ferry MV *Magallanes* between the mainland Chilean city of Puerto Montt and Puerto Natales. The boat normally leaves Puerto Montt Monday and arrives in Puerto Natales on Thursday morning. Early in the peak summer season, it's fairly easy to get a northbound berth, but later in the season reservations are advisable. Fares depend on the season and quality of accommodations but range US$275–1,720 pp with full board. Vehicles (including bikes) cost extra.

Northbound sailing day is usually Friday at 6 A.M., but weather and tides can change schedules. Passengers normally spend the night on board before these early-morning departures, but Navimag also has a Sala de Espera (waiting room) immediately across from the new pier.

### GETTING AROUND

**Emsa/Avis** (Bulnes 632, tel. 061/410775), **MotorCars** (Blanco Encalada 330, tel. 061/413593), and **Express Rentacar** (Bulnes 28-B, tel. 061, 412109, www.express-rentacar.com) rent cars, but there's a wider selection in Punta Arenas. **World's End** (Blanco Encalada 226, tel. 061/414725) rents bicycles and motorcycles. **Path@gone** (Eberhard 599, tel./fax 061/413290) also rents bicycles.

# Vicinity of Puerto Natales

A growing number of operators arrange excursions to nearby sites of interest and, of course, to Parque Nacional Torres del Paine and even Argentina's Parque Nacional Los Glaciares.

Several operators have organized complementary, one-stop arrangements for Torres del Paine under the umbrella of **Path@gone** (Eberhard 599, tel./fax 061/413290, www.pathagone.com). These include **Andescape** (tel./fax 061/412592, www.andescape.cl); **Fantástico Sur** (Magallanes 960, Punta Arenas, tel. 061/710050, www.lastorres.com); **Onas Aventura Patagonia** (tel./fax 061/412707, www.onaspatagonia.com), which also does sea kayaking, trekking, and full-day excursions to Paine; and **Turismo Stipe** (tel./fax 061/411125, turismostipe@entelchile.net).

Other agencies include **Antares Patagonia Adventure** (Barros Arana 111, tel. 061/414611, www.antarespatagonia.com) for sea kayaking in particular; **Big Foot Adventure Patagonia** (Bories 206, tel. 061/414611, fax 061/414276, www.bigfootpatagonia.com) for sea kayaking, trekking, ice hiking, climbing, mountaineering, and more general excursions as well; **Chile Nativo** (Eberhard 230, tel. 061/411385, fax 061/415474, www.chilenativo.com) for riding, trekking, and bird-watching; and **Servitur**

(Prat 353, tel./fax 061/411858, servitur@entelchile.net). **Baqueano Zamora** (Baquedano 534, tel. 061/413953, www.baqueanozamora.com) specializes in horseback trips in the park and is also the concessionaire for Posada Río Serrano and Hostería El Pionero.

## FRIGORÍFICO BORIES

Only four kilometers north of Puerto Natales, the Sociedad Explotadora de Tierra del Fuego built this state-of-the-art (for its time) meat freezer to prepare excess livestock, primarily sheep, for shipment to Europe. Built of brick masonry between 1912 and 1914, in the Magellanic style, it's the only plant of its kind in a reasonable state of preservation. After expropriation by the Allende government in 1971, the plant was partially dismantled and finally shut down a few years back.

Among the remaining structures are the rendering plant, which converted animal fat into tallow, the tannery that prepared hides for shipment, and the main offices, smithery, locomotive repair shop (Bories had its own short line), freight jetty, power plant, and boilers. The power plant still works.

Accommodations and food are available at **Hotel Cisne Cuello Negro** (tel. 061/411498, US$110/134 s/d); make reservations through **Turismo Pehoé** (José Menéndez 918, Punta Arenas, tel. 061/244506, ventas@pehoe.cl). Rates include private bath and breakfast; there is also a restaurant.

## PUERTO PRAT AND VICINITY

About 15 kilometers northwest of Puerto Natales via a gravel road, sheltered Puerto Prat is the nearest thing to a beach getaway that Natalinos have—on rare hot days, its shallow waters warm up enough to let the truly intrepid dip their toes into the sea. It is also the paddling point for one-day sea kayak trips to **Fiordo Eberhard** (US$120 pp); for details, contact Big Foot Adventure Patagonia in Puerto Natales.

A short distance north, settled by Captain Hermann Eberhard, **Estancia Puerto Consuelo** was the area's first sheep farm. It's

open to the public, but usually only those on horseback excursions.

## DIFUNTA CORREA SHRINE

About six kilometers east of Puerto Natales, on the south side of Ruta 9, the spreading mountain of water-filled plastic bottles at this spontaneous roadside shrine suggests one of two things: either many Argentines are traveling here, or Chileans are becoming devoted to Argentina's favorite folk saint. Or it may be a changing combination of the two, as the recent Argentine economic crisis reversed the traditional flow of Argentine tourists into Chile.

## CERRO DOROTEA

About seven kilometers east of town on Ruta 9, nudging the Argentine border, the hike to the Sierra Dorotea ridge makes an ideal half-day excursion, offering some of the area's finest panoramas. Well-marked with red blazes and signs, the route to Cerro Dorotea's 549-meter summit is, after the initial approach,

The Argentine folk saint Difunta Correa has a large roadside shrine near Puerto Natales.

unrelentingly uphill but never exhaustingly steep. This is not pristine nature—much of the lower slopes are cutover *lenga* forest, some of which has regenerated itself into an even-aged woodland. The ridge itself is barren, with a telephone relay antenna on the top.

Trailhead access is over private property, where farmer Juan de Dios Saavedra Ortiz collects US$7.50 per person. The fee, though, includes a simple but welcome Chilean *onces* (afternoon tea with homemade bread, butter, ham, and cheese) on your return from the hike.

## MONUMENTO NATURAL CUEVA DEL MILODÓN

Northwest of present-day Puerto Natales, on the shores of a small inlet known as Fiordo Eberhard, the giant Pleistocene ground sloth known as the mylodon (*Mylodon darwini*) took shelter in this wave-cut grotto some 30 meters high and 80 meters wide at its mouth, and 200 meters deep. While the mylodon has been extinct for nearly as long as humans have inhabited the area—some 11,000 years ago—the discovery of its remains caused a sensation in Europe, as their state of preservation induced some scientists to speculate the animal might still be alive.

German pioneer sheep farmer Hermann Eberhard gets credit for discovering the cave in 1895, but Erland Nordenskjöld (1900) was the first scientist to study it, taking sample bones and skin back to Sweden. Its manure has been carbon-dated at roughly 10,400 years before the present, meaning the large herbivore coexisted with humans, but it was most definitely *not* a domesticate. In all probability, though, hunting pressure contributed to its demise (and that of many other Pleistocene megafauna). Oddly enough, no complete skeleton has been found.

The mylodon has gained a spot in the Western imagination, both among scientists and the lay public. U.S. archaeologist Junius Bird described the animal in his journals, published as *Travel and Archaeology in South Chile* (University of Iowa Press, 1988), edited by John Hyslop of the American Museum of Natural History. Family tales inspired Bruce Chatwin to write his masterpiece *In Patagonia*, which relates far-fetched legends that Paleo-Indians penned the mylodon in the cave and that some animals survived into the 19th century.

Conaf's **Museo de Sitio,** open 8 A.M.–8 P.M. daily, has excellent information on the 192-hectare park, which attracted nearly 46,000 visitors in 2003, more than half of them Chilean. A tacky life-size statue of the mylodon stands in the cave itself.

Summer admission costs US$5.50 for adult foreigners, US$2.75 for Chilean residents, with nominal rates for children. Many Natales-based tours take in the sight, but there is no regular public transport except for Paine-bound buses that pass on Ruta 9, five kilometers east. Mountain-bike rental could be a good option. In addition to the park's picnic area, there's now a good restaurant nearby.

## GLACIAR BALMACEDA (PARQUE NACIONAL BERNARDO O'HIGGINS)

Chile's largest national park, covering 3,525,901 hectares of islands and icecaps from near Tortel in Region XI (Aisén) to Última Esperanza in Region XII (Magallanes), has few easy access points, but the Balmaceda glacier at the Río Serrano's outlet is one of them. From Puerto Natales, the closest approach is a four-hour sail northwest—where Juan Ladrilleros and Pedro de Sarmiento de Gamboa ended their futile quests for a sheltered route to the Pacific—past Puerto Bories, several wool *estancias* reachable only by sea, and nesting colonies of seabirds and breeding colonies of southern sea lions, among U-shaped valleys with glaciers and waterfalls. Andean condors have been sighted in the area.

At the end of the cruise, passengers disembark for an hour or so at **Puerto Toro,** where a half-hour walk through southern beech forest leads to the fast-receding **Glaciar Balmaceda.** Visitors remain about an hour before returning to Natales, unless they take advantage of the option to travel upriver to Torres del Paine, which may be visible in the distance.

A new option for visiting remote parts of the park, in comfort, is the five-day, four-night

Skorpios cruise of the so-called Ruta Kawéskar. For more detail, contact Cruceros Skorpios (Agustín Leguía Norte 118, Las Condes, Santiago, Chile, tel. 56-2/4771900, www. Skorpios.cl).

## Accommodations and Food

There are no formal accommodations in the park. Across the sound from Puerto Toro, though, in virtually the most peaceful location imaginable—but for the wind—the nearly new **Hostería Monte Balmaceda** (c/o Turismo 21 de Mayo, Eberhard 560, Puerto Natales, tel. 061/411978, 21demayo@chileaustral.com) charges US$105/140 s/d with breakfast.

Almost alongside the hostería, **Refugio Monte Balmaceda** (US$25 pp) is a comfortable tent-style hostel (sleeping bags not provided) with shared baths. Guests at both the *hostería* and the *refugio* can lunch or sup at the restaurant for US$18 per person.

As it's mostly accessible by sea, a stay here is usually part of a package including a visit to the park and/or Torres del Paine. There is, however, a footpath suitable for a two-day trek to or from Torres del Paine.

## Getting There

Several Natales operators sail up the sound to the Balmaceda glacier, usually daily in summer, less frequently the rest of the year. Bad weather and high winds may cause cancellations at any time of year.

**Turismo 21 de Mayo** (Eberhard 560, tel. 061/411978, 21demayo@chileaustral.com) sails its eponymous cutter or the yacht *Alberto de Agostini* to the park. Fares are US$60 per person; on the return the boat stops at Estancias Los Perales, where there's an optional *asado* for US$12 per person.

A new entrant is the far faster *Catamarán Fiordos del Sur,* operated by **Turismo Runner** (Eberhard 555, tel. 061/712132, www.turismorunner.cl), at 8 A.M. and 2 P.M. daily in summer, less frequently the rest of the year. At US$67, it's slightly more expensive than the slower boats, but a good alternative for those with limited time.

Instead of returning to Puerto Natales, it's possible to continue upriver to Torres del Paine with either 21 de Mayo or with **Onas Patagonia** (Eberhard 599, tel. 061/414349, tel./fax 061/412707, www.onaspatagonia.com). In open Zodiac rafts, supplying all passengers with warm wet-weather gear, Onas passes scenic areas not normally seen by visitors to Paine, makes a lunch stop along the Río Serrano, and requires a brief portage around the Serrano rapids before arriving at the Río Serrano campground. The total cost is US$90; the excursion can also be done in the opposite direction.

## CERRO CASTILLO AND VICINITY

North of Natales, one of Chile's most thinly populated municipalities, the *comuna* of Torres del Paine has only 739 inhabitants by the 2002 census; more than half reside in the hamlet of Cerro Castillo, 60 kilometers north of Puerto Natales on Ruta 9, alongside the Río Don Guillermo border crossing. Called Cancha Carrera on the Argentine side, this is the most direct route from Parque Nacional Torres del Paine to El Calafate (Argentina) and Parque Nacional Los Glaciares. Formerly seasonal, it is now open all year.

Formerly an *estancia* belonging to the powerful Sociedad Explotadora de Tierra del Fuego, Cerro Castillo has an assortment of services, including a dismal museum at the municipal **Departamento de Turismo** (Avenida Bernardo O'Higgins s/n, tel. 061/691932) and the only gas station north of Puerto Natales (if continuing to Argentina, though, fuel is much cheaper on the Argentine side).

En route to and at Cerro Castillo, there are several accommodations options. The most southerly, **Hostería Patagonia Inn** (Km 26 Norte, Sector Dos Lagunas, tel. 061/228117 or 061/415153, www.patagoniainn.com, US$42/55 s/d) is a former Braun-Menéndez property and its own small museum still holds some of the *estancia's* record books. For the price, its 15 rooms with private bath, central heating, and TV offer good value; it also has a restaurant.

On the site of an older namesake that burned

to the ground, **Hotel Tres Pasos** (Km 38 Norte, tel. 02/1969630 or 02/1969631, www .hotel3pasos.cl, US$111/137 s/d) is a contemporary roadside inn that's well above average for the area. Lunch or dinner costs US$17 at its restaurant.

At Cerro Castillo itself, there are basic accommodations at **Residencial Loreto Belén** (tel. 061/691932, Anexo 728, US$19 pp) and more elaborate lodgings at **Hostería El Pionero** (tel. 061/413953, tel./fax 061/412911, baqueanoz@terra.cl, US$25 pp, US$111/130 s/d); the cheaper rooms belong to an annex *refugio*. Open September–April only, it also serves meals to nonguests and rents horses.

On Estancia Cerro Guido, about midway between Cerro Castillo and Torres del Paine,

**Lodge Cerro Guido** (tel. 02/1964807, lodge@ cerroguido.cl, US$155/176 s/d) has rehabbed and modernized its historic *casco* and another structure, on what is still a working sheep ranch, into attractive guesthouses with ten total rooms. About 12 kilometers north of the road that leads to the park's Laguna Amarga entrance, Cerro Guido gets far less traffic than Paine's accommodations, but its facilities equal or better most of them; there's also a restaurant/bar whose wines come from the ownership's own Matetic family vineyards between Santiago and Valparaíso. Rates include breakfast, while lunch or dinner costs US$30 extra. Activities include horseback riding (multiday excursions are possible), hiking, and observing farm activities such as summer shearing.

# Parque Nacional Torres del Paine

Several years ago, when a major Pacific Coast shipping company placed a two-page ad in Alaska Airlines' in-flight magazine, the landscape chosen to represent Alaska's grandeur was…Parque Nacional Torres del Paine! While an uninformed photo editor was the likely culprit—ironically enough for a Southern Hemisphere destination, the image was reversed—the soaring granite spires of Chile's premiere national park have truly become an international emblem of alpine majesty.

But there's more—unlike many South American parks, Torres del Paine has an integrated network of hiking trails suitable for day-trips and backpack treks, endangered species such as the wild guanaco in a UNESCO-recognized World Biosphere Reserve, and accommodations options ranging from rustic campgrounds to cozy trail huts and five-star luxury hotels. So popular that some visitors prefer the shoulder seasons of spring (Nov.– Dec.) or fall (Mar.–Apr.)—the park receives more than 100,000 visitors annually, about three-quarters of them foreigners. While Torres del Paine has become a major international destination, it's still wild country.

Nearly everybody visits the park to behold extraordinary natural features such as the **Torres del Paine,** the sheer granite towers that defy erosion even as the weaker sedimentary strata around them have weathered, and the jagged **Cuernos del Paine,** with their striking interface between igneous and metamorphic rocks. Most hike its trails uneventfully, but for all its popularity, this can still be treacherous terrain. Hikers have disappeared, the rivers run fast and cold, the weather is unpredictable, and there is one documented case of a tourist killed by a puma.

## ORIENTATION

Parque Nacional Torres del Paine is 112 kilometers northwest of Puerto Natales via Ruta 9 through Cerro Castillo; 38 kilometers beyond Castillo, a westbound lateral traces the southern shore of Lago Sarmiento de Gamboa to the park's isolated Laguna Verde sector. Three kilometers beyond the Laguna Verde junction, another westbound lateral leaves Ruta 9 to follow Lago Sarmiento's north shore to Portería Sarmiento, the main gate; it continues southwest for 37 kilometers to the Administración, the park headquarters at the west end of Lago del Toro.

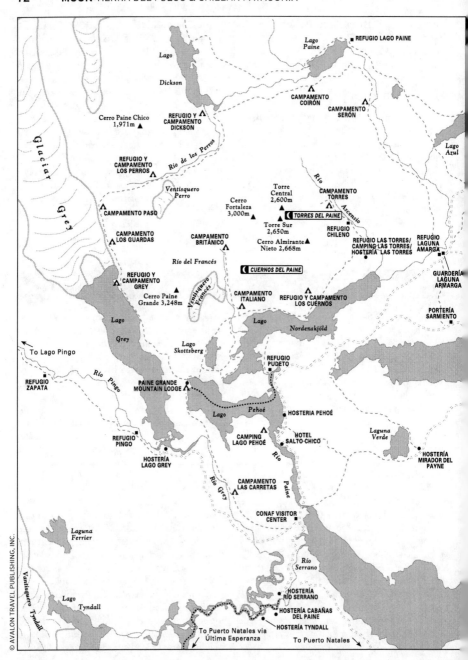

CAMPING
LAGUNA AZUL

GUARDERÍA
LAGUNA AZUL

# PARQUE NACIONAL
# TORRES DEL PAINE

Laguna
Amarga

Lago    Sarmiento

Sierra   del   Toro

To Cerro Castillo
and Puerto Natales

Lago   Toro

0                    4 mi

0          4 km

Twelve kilometers east of Portería Sarmiento, another lateral branches northwest and, three kilometers farther on, splits again; the former leads to Guardería Laguna Azul, in the little-visited northern sector, while the latter enters the park at Guardería Laguna Amarga, the most common starting point for the popular Paine Circuit, and follows the south shore of Lago Nordenskjöld and Lago Pehoé en route to the Administración visitors center. Most public transportation takes this route.

Recently completed, a new bridge over the Río Serrano will soon permit access to park headquarters via Cueva del Milodón and Lago del Toro's western shore. It remains to be seen how this will affect public transportation.

## GEOGRAPHY AND CLIMATE

Parque Nacional Torres del Paine comprises 181,414 hectares of Patagonian steppe, low-land and alpine glacial lakes, glacier-fed torrents and waterfalls, forested uplands, and nearly vertical granite needles. Altitudes range from only about 50 meters above sea level along the lower Río Serrano to 3,050 meters atop Paine Grande, the central massif's tallest peak.

Paine has a cool temperate climate characterized by frequent high winds, especially in spring and summer. The average summer temperature is about 10.8°C, with maxima reaching around 23°C, while the average winter minimum is around freezing. Average figures are misleading, though, as the weather is highly changeable. The park lies in the rain shadow of the Campo de Hielo Sur, where westerly storms drop most of their load as snow, so it receives only about 600 millimeters rainfall per annum. Still, snow and hail can fall even in midsummer. Spring is probably the windiest time; in autumn, March and April, winds tend to moderate, but days are shorter.

It should go without saying that at higher elevations temperatures are cooler and snow is likelier to fall. In some areas it's possible to hut-hop between *refugios,* eliminating the need for a tent and sleeping bag—but not for warm clothing and impermeable raingear.

## FLORA AND FAUNA

Less diverse than in areas farther north, Paine's vegetation still varies with altitude and distance from the Andes. Bunch grasses of the genera *Festuca* and *Stipa,* known collectively as *coirón,* cover the park's arid southeastern steppes, often interspersed with thorny shrubs such as the *calafate (Berberis buxifolia),* which produces edible fruit, and *neneo (Anathrophillum desideratum).* There are also miniature ground-hugging orchids such as the *zapatito (Calceolaria uniflora)* and *capachito (Calceolaria biflora).*

Approaching the Andes, deciduous forests of *lenga (Nothofagus pumilio)* blanket the hillsides, along with the evergreen *coigue de Magallanes (Nothofagus betuloides)* and the deciduous *ñirre (Nothofagus antarctica).* At the highest elevations, little vegetation of any kind grows among the alpine fell fields.

Among Paine's mammals, the most conspicuous is the guanaco (*Lama guanicoe*), whose numbers—and tameness—have increased dramatically over the past two decades. Many of its young, known as *chulengos,* fall prey to the puma (*Felis concolor*). A more common predator, or at least a more visible one, is the gray fox (*Dusicyon griseus*), which feeds off the introduced European hare and, beyond park boundaries, off sheep. The endangered *huemul* or Andean deer (*Hippocamelus bisulcus*) is a rare sight.

The monarch of South American birds, of course, is the Andean condor (*Vultur gryphus*), not a rare sight here. Filtering the lake shallows for plankton, the Chilean flamingo (*Phoenicopterus chilensis*) summers here after breeding in the northern altiplano. The *caiquén* or upland goose (*Chloephaga picta*) grazes the moist grasslands around the lakes, while the black-necked swan (*Cygnus melancoryphus*) paddles peacefully on the surface. The fleet but flightless rhea or *ñandú (Pterocnemia pennata)* scampers over the steppes.

## ◖ TORRES DEL PAINE

Some of the Andes' youngest peaks, the Torres del Paine are among the most emblematic in the entire range. Some 10 million years ago, a magma intrusion failed to reach the earth's surface, cooling underground into resistant granite; in the interim, water, ice, and snow have eroded softer surrounding terrain to liberate the spires of Torres del Paine into one of South America's most dramatic landscapes.

So strong a draw are the Torres that some visitors pressed for time settle for day tours that allow only a few hours in the park. Many others walk to the base of the Torres from Hostería Las Torres, a relatively easy day hike where it's hard to avoid the crowds. A longer and more tiring alternative, up the steep canyon of the Río Bader, provides a different perspective and the solitude that many hikers seek in the mountains.

## ◖ CUERNOS DEL PAINE

Many visitors to the park misidentify the Cuernos del Paine (Horns of Paine) as the Torres. Located almost immediately south of the Torres proper, the saw-toothed Cuernos retain a cap of darker but softer metamorphic rock atop a broader granitic batholith that, like the Torres, never reached the surface before cooling. It's the sharp contrast between the two that gives the Cuernos their striking aspect.

As with the Torres, day-trippers can admire the Cuernos from the highway through the park. The best views, though, come from the "W" trail along the north shore of Lago Nordenskjöld, between Hostería Las Torres and Lago Pehoé.

## HIKING THE PAINE CIRCUIT

More than two decades ago, under a military dictatorship, Chile attracted few foreign visitors, and hiking in Torres del Paine was a solitary experience—on a 10-day trek over the now famous Paine circuit, the author met only three other hikers, two Americans and a Chilean. Parts of the route were easy-to-follow stock trails (the park was once an *estancia*), while others, on the east shore of Lago Grey and into the valley of the Río de los Perros in particular, were barely boot-width tracks on steep slopes, or involved scrambling over granite boulders and fording waist-deep glacial meltwater.

In the interim, as raging rivers have destroyed bridges at the outlets of Lago Nordenskjöld and Lago Paine, the original trailhead on Lago Pehoé's north shore no longer exists. Meanwhile, completion of a trail along Lago Nordenskjöld's north shore several years back created a new loop and simultaneously provided access to the south side of the Torres, offering easier access up the Río Ascencio and Valle del Francés in what is often done as the shorter "W" route to Lago Pehoé. Where the former circuit crossed the Río Paine and continued along its north bank to the Laguna Azul campground, the new circuit now follows the river's west bank south to Laguna Amarga (a Laguna Azul exit or entrance is still feasible, though, by crossing the Río Paine by a cable raft at the river's Lago Dickson outlet, with help from the staff at Refugio Dickson).

In the interim, trail maintenance and development have improved, rudimentary and not-so-rudimentary bridges have replaced fallen logs and traversed stream fords, and comfortable concessionaire *refugios* and organized campgrounds have supplanted the lean-tos and *puestos* (outside houses) that once sheltered shepherds on their rounds. Though it's theoretically possible to complete most of the circuit without a tent or even a sleeping bag, showering and eating at the *refugios,* hikers must not forget that this is still rugged country with unpredictable weather.

Most hikers now tackle the circuit counterclockwise from Guardería Laguna Amarga, where buses from Puerto Natales stop for passengers to pay the park admission fee. An alternative is to continue to Pudeto and take a passenger launch to Refugio Pehoé, or else to the park's Administración (involving a longer and less interesting approach); both of these mean doing the trek clockwise.

At least a week is desirable for the circuit; before beginning, registration with park rangers is obligatory. Camping is permitted only at designated sites, a few of which are free. Purchase supplies in Puerto Natales, as only limited goods are available with the park, at premium prices.

## Accommodations and Food

For counterclockwise hikers beginning at Laguna Amarga, there is no *refugio* until Lago Dickson (roughly 11 hours), though there is a fee campground at **Campamento Serón** (4–5 hours).

Under Conaf concession to Puerto Natales's **Andescape** (Eberhard 599, tel. 061/412877, andescape@terra.cl) are **Refugio Lago Grey** and **Refugio Lago Dickson,** where there are also campgrounds and backpackers still crash at the old *puesto,* plus the **Campamento Río de los Perros.**

Both these *refugios* resemble each other, with 32 bunks charging US$25 per person, with kitchen privileges and hot showers, but without sheets or sleeping bags, which are available for rental but sometimes scarce. Breakfast costs US$8.50, lunch US$13, dinner US$15; a bunk with full board costs US$59 per person. Campers pay US$6.50 each (*refugio* guests, though, have shower priority). Rental tents, sleeping bags, mats, and campstoves are also available.

Replacing the cramped and traditionally overcrowded Refugio Lago Pehoé, the **Paine Grande Mountain Lodge** is the newest option along the Paine Circuit; make reservations through Turismo Comapa (Bulnes 533, tel. 061/414300, Puerto Natales, www.comapa .cl). Rates are US$35 per person without breakfast (US$9 extra); lunch (US$12) and dinner (US$15) are available separately, but full-board packages (US$63 pp) mean a small savings. Camping costs US$6.50 pp, and there's also phone and even Internet access.

## HIKING THE "W" VARIANT

From Guardería Laguna Amarga, a narrow undulating road crosses the Río Paine on a narrow bridge to the grounds of **Estancia Cerro Paine,** beneath the 2,640-meter summit of Monte Almirante Nieto. The *estancia* operates a hotel, *refugios,* and campgrounds, and also shuttles hikers back and forth from Laguna Amarga for US$4 per person.

From Estancia Cerro Paine, a northbound trail parallels the route from Guardería Laguna Amarga, eventually meeting it just south of

Campamento Serón. The *estancia* is more notable, though, as the starting point for the "W" route to Lago Pehoé, a scenic and popular option for hikers lacking time for the full circuit. On the western edge of the *estancia* grounds, the trail crosses the Río Ascencio on a footbridge to a junction where a northbound lateral climbs the river canyon to Campamento Torres, where a short but very steep trail ascends to a nameless, glacial tarn at the foot of the Torres proper. This is an easy day hike from the *estancia*, though many people prefer to camp or spend the night at the *refugio*.

From the junction, the main trail follows Lago Nordenskjöld's north shore, past another *refugio* and campground, to the free Campamento Italiano at the base of the **Río del Francés** valley. While the main trail continues west toward Lago Pehoé, another northbound lateral climbs steeply up the valley, between the striking metamorphic Cuernos del Paine to the east and the 3,050-meter granite summit of Paine Grande to the west, to the free Campamento Británico.

Hikers in search of peace and quiet can make a strenuous detour up the **Valle Bader,** a steep rugged river valley that's home to a climber's camp at the base of the Cuernos. This involves a very stiff climb, and the route is mostly unmarked, but experienced cross-country walkers can handle it.

## Accommodations and Food

Technically outside park boundaries, most of the "W" route along Lago Nordenskjöld's north shore belongs to **Fantástico Sur** (José Menéndez 858, Departamento 4, Punta Arenas, tel./fax 061/247194, www.lastorres.com), which runs the 96-bunk **Refugio Las Torres Norte** and the new, nearby **Refugio Las Torres Central** on the *estancia*'s main grounds; the 36-bunk **Refugio Chileno** in the upper Río Ascencio valley; and the 28-bunk **Refugio Los Cuernos,** all of which also have campgrounds. Fantástico Sur's *refugios* are more spacious, diverse, and attractive in design than the Conaf *refugios,* and the food is better as well.

Bunks at Fantástico Sur *refugios* cost US$33–36 per person (US$62–67 pp with full board), while camping costs US$6.50 per person with hot showers. Refugio Los Cuernos also has two-person *cabañas* (US$43 pp, US$74 with full board).

Separately, breakfast costs US$8, lunch US$13, or dinner US$15; a full meal package costs US$35. Rental tents, sleeping bags, mats, and stoves are also available.

## OTHER TRAILS

After heavy runoff destroyed the once-sturdy bridge at the outlet of Lago Paine in the early 1980s, the north shore of the Río Paine became, and has remained, isolated from the rest of the park. A good road, though, still goes from Guardería Laguna Amarga to the east end of Laguna Azul, where there are a campground and *cabañas,* and the **Sendero Lago Paine,** a four-hour walk to the lake and a simple *refugio.* A trekkers' alternative is the **Sendero Desembocadura,** which leads north from Guardería Laguna Amarga through open country to the west end of Laguna Azul and continues to Lago Paine, but this takes about eight hours. From the north shore of Lago Paine, the **Sendero Lago Dickson** (5.5 hours) leads to the Dickson glacier.

Several easy day hikes are possible near Guardería Lago Pehoé, directly on the road from Laguna Amarga to the Administración visitors center. The short **Sendero Salto Grande** leads to the thunderous waterfall, at Lago Sarmiento's outlet, that was the circuit's starting point until unprecedented runoff swept away the iron bridge to Península Pehoé in 1986. From Salto Grande, the **Sendero Mirador Nordenskjöld** is a slightly longer but still easy walk to a lakeshore vista point, directly opposite the stunning Cuernos del Paine.

From Guardería Lago Grey, 18 kilometers northwest of the Administración by road, a short footpath leads to a sandy beach on Lago Grey's south shore, where steady westerlies often beach icebergs from Glaciar Grey. The longer and less visited **Sendero Lago Pingo** ascends the Río Pingo valley to its namesake lake (5.5–6 hours); there are a basic *refugio* and two free campgrounds along the route.

# MOUNTAINEERING

Though popular, hiking is not the only recreational option for Paine visitors.

Despite the similarity of terrain, Paine attracts fewer climbers than Argentina's neighboring Parque Nacional Los Glaciares, perhaps because fees for climbing permits have been very high here. At present, permits are free of charge; before being granted permission, though, climbers must present Conaf with climbing résumés, emergency contacts, and authorization from their consulate.

When climbing in sensitive border areas (meaning most of Andean Chile), climbers must also have permission from the Dirección de Fronteras y Límites (Difrol) in Santiago. It's possible to do this through a Chilean consulate overseas or at Difrol's Santiago offices; if you arrive in Puerto Natales without permission, it's possible to request it through the **Gobernación Provincial** (tel. 061/411423, fax 061/411992), the regional government offices on the south side of Plaza Arturo Prat. The turnaround time is 48 hours. Once you receive permission, you'll need to present it to Conaf and request the amount of time you want. Ask for more time than you'll need, as each separate trip to the park could require a separate fee.

While climbing and mountaineering activities may be undertaken independently, local concessionaires can provide training and lead groups or individuals with less experience on snow and ice. Puerto Natales's Big Foot Adventure Patagonia, for instance, has a Refugio Grey base camp, where it leads half-day traverses of the west side of Glaciar Grey (US$110 pp) and has longer trips up to three days (US$500). Except for warm, weather-proof clothing, they provide all equipment. For more detail, contact **Big Foot Adventure Patagonia** (Bories 206, tel./fax 061/413247, www.bigfootpatagonia.com).

# KAYAKING AND HORSEBACK RIDING

Big Foot also arranges guided three-day, two-night kayak descents of the Río Serrano for US$500 per person.

The only park concessionaire offering horse-back trips is Río Serrano–based **Baquean Zamora** (Baquedano 534, Puerto Natales, tel. 061/413953, www.baqueanozamora.com). Just outside the park boundaries, though, Hostería Las Torres (Sarmiento 846, Punta Arenas, tel. 061/360360, www.lastorres.com) has its own stables.

# ACCOMMODATIONS

Park accommodations range from free trailside campgrounds to first-rate luxury hotels with just about everything in between; in summer, reservations are almost obligatory at hotels and advisable at campgrounds and *refugios*. For options along the Paine Circuit and other trails, see the earlier descriptions.

## Camping

At Estancia Cerro Paine, **Camping Las Torres** (US$6.50 pp) draws hikers heading up the Río Ascencio valley to the Paine overlook and/or west on the "W" route to Lago Pehoé, or finishing up the circuit here. Formerly insufficient shower and toilet facilities have improved substantially.

On a bluff above Refugio Las Torres, the **Cascada Eco-Camp** is a geodesic dome-tent facility designed for minimum-impact accommodations; on raised platforms, each tent is five meters wide, with wooden floors and two single beds, and towels and bedding including down comforters. Two larger domes contain a common living area, dining rooms, and kitchen; the separate bathrooms have hot showers and composting toilets (from some domes, it's a long walk for middle-of-the-night toilet visits). Electricity comes from solar collectors, windmills, and a small hydroelectric turbine. It's open, however, only to clients of Cascada Expediciones (Don Carlos 3219, Las Condes, Santiago, Chile, tel. 56-2/2329878, U.S. tel. 800/901-6987, U.K. tel. 0-800/051-7095, www.cascada.travel).

On the small peninsula on the eastern shore of its namesake lake, just west of the road to the Administración, sites at the concessionaire-run **Camping Lago Pehoé** (tel. 02/1960377, asoto@sodexho.cl, US$26) hold up to six people; fees include firewood and hot showers.

...ometers south of park headquar-
...ing **Río Serrano** (US$6.50 pp) has
...eopened with considerable improve-
including cooking shelters at each site.
Paine's remote northeastern sector, which
...e visitors prefer, is **Camping Laguna Azul**
...el. 061/411157 in Puerto Natales, cpena@
laauracana.cl, US$22 per site).

## Refugios, Hosterías, and Hotels

Near the Administración, Conaf's inexpensive
**Refugio Lago Toro** (US$7 pp) has been closed
but may reopen; bring your own sleeping bag
and expect to pay a bit extra for hot showers.

**Posada Río Serrano** (tel. 061/413953,
baqueanoz@tie.cl, US$92–125 d) is a former
*estancia* house retrofitted as a bed-and-breakfast. Rates, which include breakfast, depend on
whether the room has shared or private bath; there
is a restaurant/bar for other meals and for drinks.
While it's improved under new management, and
quadruples and sextuples can be cheaper per person, it's overpriced for what it offers.

Reachable by road along Lago Sarmiento's
south shore or by foot or horseback from the
Río Paine, well-regarded **Hostería Mirador
del Payne** (tel. 061/410498, www.mirador
delpayne.com, US$143/176 s/d) lies in the iso-
lated southeastern Laguna Verde sector.

Where Lago Grey becomes the Río Grey, the
30-room **Hostería Lago Grey** (US$217/250
s/d with breakfast) hosts visitors to the park's
lesser-visited western sector; it also has a restaurant open to the public. For reservations,
contact them through **Turismo Runner** (Eberhard 555, Puerto Natales, tel. 061/712106,
www.lagogrey.cl).

The park's oldest hotel, on a five-hectare island linked to the mainland by a footbridge,
the 25-room **Hostería Pehoé** (US$225/260
s/d) has improved substantially since the op-
erator won a lawsuit against Conaf and began
to reinvest in what had been a rundown facility, with substandard service, in an undeniably
spectacular setting. For reservations, contact
**Turismo Pehoé** (José Menéndez 918, Punta
Arenas, tel. 061/241373, www.pehoe.com).

At Estancia Cerro Paine, seven kilometers

west of Guardería Laguna Amarga, the sprawling but well-run **( Hostería Las Torres**
(US$141/161–220/276 s/d) is one of the park's
gems for its setting beneath Monte Almirante
Nieto, its professionalism, the recent addition
of a spa, which offering saunas and massages,
and even WiFi access (expensive because of a
costly satellite link). While it's an elite option,
it's conscientiously eco-friendly in terms of
waste disposal, and management is constantly
seeking feedback from guests. Open to both
guests and nonguests, the tobacco-free restaurant prepares quality food in cruise-ship
quantities. For reservations, contact Hostería
Las Torres (Sarmiento 846, Punta Arenas, tel.
061/360360, www.lastorres.com); it now offers
all-inclusive packages as well as just lodging.
Off-season hotel rates are about half.

Open for packages only, **( Hotel Salto
Chico** is a mega-luxury resort that, some-
how, manages to blend inconspicuously into
the landscape while providing some of the
grandest views of any hotel on the globe.
Rates start at US$3,060/4,340 s/d for four
nights in the least expensive room, ranging
up to US$9,010/11,120 s/d for eight nights in
the costliest suite, including transfer to and
from Punta Arenas and unlimited park excursions. Low-season rates are about 20 percent cheaper. For details and/or reservations,
contact **Explora Hotels** (Américo Vespucio
Sur 80, 5th floor, Las Condes, Santiago, tel.
02/2066060, www.explora.com).

Just beyond park boundaries, reached by
launch over the Río Serrano, the stylish **Hotel
Lago Tyndall** (Lucas Bonacic 024, Punta Arenas, tel./fax 061/230941, www.hoteltyndall
.cl, US$157/182–196/206 s/d) enjoys peace,
quiet, and magnificent views. Nearby is the
less stylish **Hostería Cabañas del Paine** (tel.
061/220174 in Punta Arenas, cabanasdel-
paine@chileaustral.com, US$173/200 s/d).

## INFORMATION

Conaf's principal facility is its **Centro de
Informaciones Ecológicas** (tel. 061/691931,
ptpaine@conaf.cl), at the Administración
building on the shores of Lago del Toro near

the Río Paine outlet, which features good natural history exhibits. It's open 8:30 A.M.–8 P.M. daily in summer. A new visitors center is also due to open at the Lago Pehoé ranger station, the former *refugio*.

Ranger stations at Guardería Laguna Amarga, Portería Lago Sarmiento, Guardería Laguna Azul, Guardería Lago Verde, and Guardería Lago Grey can also provide information.

At the same time, the privately run Hostería Las Torres has an excellent audiovisual salon with sophisticated environmental exhibits.

### Entry Fee

For foreigners, Torres del Paine is Chile's most expensive national park—US$19 per person except May 1–September 30, when it's only half that. Rangers at Portería Lago Sarmiento, Guardería Laguna Amarga (where most inbound buses now stop), Guardería Lago Verde, or Guardería Laguna Azul collect the fee, issue receipts, and also provide a 1:100,000 park map that is suitable for trekking.

### Books and Maps

The text and coverage of the fifth edition of Tim Burford's *Chile & Argentina: The Bradt Trekking Guide* (Bradt Publications, 2001) are greatly improved over previous editions, though the maps are only so-so. Clem Lindenmayer and Nick Tapp's third edition of *Trekking in the Patagonian Andes* (Lonely Planet, 2003) has significantly better maps than Bradt and expanded coverage compared to its own previous editions. Only a few of those maps, though, are as large as the 1:100,000 scale that's desirable for hiking, though the rest are suitable for planning hikes.

Climbers should look for Alan Kearney's *Mountaineering in Patagonia* (Seattle: The Mountaineers, 1998), which includes both historical and practical information on climbing in Torres del Paine and Argentina's Parque Nacional Los Glaciares. Gladys Garay N. and Oscar Guineo N. have collaborated in *The Fauna of Torres del Paine* (1993), a locally produced guide to the park's animal life.

## GETTING THERE

Most people find the bus the cheapest and quickest way to and from the park, but the more expensive trip up Seno Última Esperanza and the Río Serrano by cutter and Zodiac is a viable and more interesting alternative. Park transportation is in flux as the new road from Puerto Natales is due to open shortly, and bus companies may adjust their routes to come more directly to the Administración, or else to take the same route (usually entering at Laguna Amarga) and loop back on the new road.

### Bus

For overland transportation details, see *Puerto Natales*. At present bus companies enter the park at Guardería Laguna Amarga, where many hikers begin the Paine circuit, before continuing to the Administración at Río Serrano. Round-trips from Natales are slightly cheaper, but companies do not accept each others' tickets.

In summer only, there may be direct bus service to El Calafate, Argentina, the closest town to that country's Parque Nacional Los Glaciares. Inquire in Puerto Natales at Calafate Travel (Baquedano 459, tel. 061/414456), though it's uncertain this office will continue.

### River

Transportation up and down the Río Serrano, between the park and Puerto Natales, has become a popular if more expensive alternative than the bus; for details, see the separate entry for Parque Nacional Bernardo O'Higgins and the Balmaceda glacier. Visitors who only want to see this sector of the river, without continuing to Puerto Natales, can do so as a day trip to Puerto Toro and back.

## GETTING AROUND

Buses to and from Puerto Natales will also carry passengers along the main park road, but as their schedules are similar, there are substantial blocks of time with no public transportation. Hitching is common, but competition is heavy and most vehicles are full with families.

There is a regular shuttle between Guardería Laguna Amarga and Estancia Cerro Paine (Hostería Las Torres, US$2 pp) that meets arriving and departing buses.

October–April, reliable transportation is available from Pudeto to Refugio Pehoé (US$19 one way, 30 minutes; US$33 round-trip) with the catamaran *Hielos Patagónicos* (tel. 061/411380 in Puerto Natales). In October and April, there is one departure daily, at noon, from Pudeto, returning at 12:30 P.M. In November and mid-March–April, there are departures at noon and 6 P.M., returning at 12:30 and 6:30 P.M. December–mid-March, there is another departure at 9:30 A.M., returning at 10 A.M. Schedules may be postponed or canceled due to bad weather, and there are no services on Christmas and New Year's Day.

Also in season, the catamaran *Grey II* goes daily from Hotel Lago Grey to Glaciar Grey (US$34 one-way, US$78 round-trip) at 9 A.M. and 3 P.M. daily; on the return, it cruises the face of the glacier, so the reverse direction costs US$52 one-way. There is a US$13 shuttle between the Administración and Hotel Lago Grey that connects with the excursion.

## MOON TIERRA DEL FUEGO
## & CHILEAN PATAGONIA

Avalon Travel
a member of the Perseus Books Group
1700 4th Street
Berkeley, CA 94710, USA
www.moon.com

Editor: Cinnamon Hearst
Series Manager: Kathryn Ettinger
Copy Editor: Amy Scott
Graphics Coordinator: Tabitha Lahr
Production Coordinator: Elizabeth Jang
Cover Designer: Tabitha Lahr
Map Editor: Albert Angulo
Cartographers: Chris Markiewicz, Kat Bennett,
   Suzanne Service, Aaron Lui
Cartography Director: Mike Morgenfeld
Proofreader: Valerie Sellers Blanton

ISBN-10: 1-59880-269-0
ISBN-13: 978-1-59880-269-6

# ABOUT THE AUTHOR

## Wayne Bernhardson

Wayne Bernhardson first traveled to Argentina in 1979 – during a military dictatorship – and has stuck with the country through good times and bad, returning repeatedly to broaden his knowledge and appreciation of the country. He owns an apartment in Buenos Aires near the Palermo botanical gardens and spends four to five months in South America every year.

Before writing best-selling guidebooks to the "Southern Cone" countries, Wayne earned a Ph.D. in Geography at the University of California, Berkeley, but abandoned academia for a nearly perpetual South American road trip. He is also author of Moon Handbooks to Buenos Aires, Chile, and Patagonia.

In addition, Wayne has written for magazines and newspapers including Trips, the San Francisco Chronicle, the American Geographical Society's Focus, Business Traveler, National Geographic Traveler, Latin Trade, Travel Holiday, and Voyageur. He often gives slide lectures on destinations he covers in his books.

When not in South America, Wayne lives in Oakland, California, with his wife María Laura Massolo; his daughter Clio Bernhardson-Massolo; and their Alaskan Malamute, Malbec (named for Argentina's signature red wine). Wayne can be reached directly by email at southerncone@mac.com or through www.guidebookwriters.com.